Indomitable

A Visually Impaired Man's Inspiring Memoir of Independence and International Achievement

Indomitable

A Visually Impaired Man's Inspiring Memoir of Independence and International Achievement

Shiro Iwae, PT, DPT

Publishing support provided by
Ignite Press
55 Shaw Ave. Suite 204
Clovis, CA 93612
www.IgnitePress.us

ISBN: 979-8-9924603-0-8
ISBN: 979-8-9924603-1-5 (E-book)
ISBN: 979-8-9924603-2-2 (Hardcover)

For bulk purchases and for booking, contact:
Shiro Iwae
shiro@driwae.com
https://driwae.com

Library of Congress Control Number: 2024927533

Cover design by Lilik Hariawan
Edited by Cathy Cruise
Interior design by Jetlaunch

FIRST EDITION

I dedicate this book to my beloved triplets, William, Garrett, and Yvonne. They grew up not knowing that their father's childhood, teenage years, and young adulthood were filled with worries, regrets, humility, and all the emotions they have experienced so far in their lives. I sincerely hope they enjoy reading this memoir of Dad's adventurous journey.

Table of Contents

To My Reader

This book contains the secrets of success. As I started pursuing my life's work, I was unaware of the existence of a proven formula that would intuitively help me achieve my dream. Now I would like to share the journey of how I reached it.

Have you ever wondered about what to do with your life? Have you ever felt that your dream was beyond your capabilities? Have you ever been envious of someone's achievement or lifestyle? Have you ever failed and lost hope?

This book will help you organize your thoughts and inspire you to achieve a bright future. Some people may realize the secret in Chapter 1; others might recognize it after reading the section titled "Exercises for Your Dream."

My discovery of this great universal truth may help you achieve a fulfilling and successful life. As you start pursuing your dream, please practice and act on the following:

"Genuinely ask for what you need and want and appreciate the help and opportunities you receive. Be generous to others and give back more than what you've been given."

Introduction

I was born on February 1, 1960, as the last child in the Iwae family in Tokyo, Japan. I was raised with a grandmother, my parents, two older brothers, and one sister; we were quite an ordinary family of seven. My father ran a small business processing and selling rice. My mother was a nurse and midwife. For most of her working life, she also worked for a company called Yakult, producing and selling drinks that improved intestinal health.

Both of my parents lived through World War II. My father was in North China when the war ended, and he was taken to a detention facility as a prisoner of war in Siberia. My mother and her adopted mother, who was also a nurse and midwife, survived the great Tokyo air raids by running away from the falling bombs that rained down fire and destruction.

Although their experiences sounded awful, I was always fascinated by the way both of my parents told their wartime stories with a bit of humor. For example, when a Russian officer came to my father's detention facility to look for someone who could play a snare drum in their military band, my father raised his hand despite never having played this instrument in his entire life. In this way, he was able to avoid hard labor. My mother recalled how she used to watch the bombs coming down for a moment before realizing that she had to run. This was because they looked like sparklers twinkling down in the night sky. "It was so pretty," she said.

On August 15, 1945, the war ended. My father was 25 and my mother was 20 years old.

Although I was diagnosed with optic neuropathy at the age of four, meaning that I would be legally blind for the rest of my life, I was able to graduate from a regular public elementary school. Between the mid-1960s and -1970s, Japan was experiencing hyper economic growth. My town, West Shinjuku, experienced a tall commercial and office building construction boom, during which skyscrapers were constructed. When I was in third grade, my new seven-story school building was completed with a planetarium on the top of it. I remember how I used to sleep during the twice-a-year planetarium presentation. I instinctively knew that I didn't have as much physical strength as my classmates, so

I had to recuperate from school activities however I could. I guess that I already had signs of what was later found to be an incurable disease called Spinocerebellar Degeneration (SCD).

Bullying was a universal phenomenon. My elementary school was no exception. A classmate who walked by me in a school hallway would call out, for no reason, "Hey, blind boy, what are you looking at?" I was called all types of names, even by professional adults. However, I was not concerned about those disrespectful people because I believed they would never be truly become successful and happy in their lives.

Most people—teachers, classmates, and neighbors—treated me with consideration. Overall, I had a very happy childhood surrounded by my grandmother, who gave me unconditional love, my parents, who tried their best to create a good family with harmony and laughter, and the rest of my siblings, who were far ahead of me in age. For example, my oldest brother had already graduated from high school and my sister was in middle school when I was just eight years old.

While I quietly observed my families' successes and failures, I developed my own philosophy of how to live well. I learned the significance of philanthropic work from my grandmother, who went beyond her calling in society. She received two medals of honor from the emperor and prime minister of Japan. She was recognized for her lifetime contributions as a midwife before, during, and after World War II. She was one of the busiest people in town, helping to educate women about the importance of prenatal care all the way through postnatal care. She told me that she helped give birth to 8,000 babies in her 50-year career. Her life sounded so tumultuous, but I was fascinated by listening to her stories while putting my head on her lap in her small yet peaceful bedroom.

No one could possibly imagine that I could go through the vigorous process of taking many liberal arts and science classes, as well as a specialized field of study in English, and then make my career in such a highly competitive country as the United States. My academic performance was a C average at best. However, I was respected and popular because I was considerate and sensitive toward others. Besides, I had a good sense of humor. I once received the biggest laugh and applause in a school play. And I played drums in a band during the middle to high school years, so I used to receive a lot of chocolates and gifts from girls at school.

This book illustrates how I intuitively followed proven principles of success during the first nine years of my unforgettable college experience to become a physical therapist.

Chapter 1

DEFINITE PURPOSE — The Beginning of All Your Achievements

"Compared to what we ought to be," said the famous professor William James of Harvard, *"we are only half awake. We are making use of only a small part of our physical and mental resources. Stating the thing broadly, the human individual thus lives far within his limits. He possesses powers of various sorts, which he habitually fails to use."*

Therefore, he crosses the largest ocean to achieve self-discovery and further possibilities.

Mother and My Undefeatable Spirit

I was born with optic neuropathy, and my eyesight was unable to be corrected by glasses or contact lenses. As a child, my eyesight measured 20/200, which categorized me as legally blind. Also, I instinctively felt that I didn't have muscle strength or endurance compared with other school friends. The differences in my overall physical abilities became rather obvious as I went through puberty and young adulthood. This condition was later found to be Spinocerebellar Degeneration (SCD), which is an incurable disease caused by genetic conditions.

My mother used to put in twice as much as work in a day so that she could take me to a recommended ophthalmologist. I was only four years old, but I sensed that she was desperate to find out the details of my eye condition because my brother, who was seven years older, likely had the same condition. The only difference regarding our visual acuity at that time was that he had to learn brail by transferring to a school for the blind when he was in the second grade. However, I was able to read school textbooks and finish at a regular elementary school. I couldn't imagine how heartbreaking it must have been to have two children called "disabled," especially in 1950s and '60s. My mother was a strong, optimistic, playful, loving, bright, and dignified woman. There are not enough words to describe her. To me, she was the earth itself.

When I was six years old, I went with my best friend for a bicycle ride. We came up a narrow street and stopped before we crossed a 25-foot-wide street. I was thinking that I had crossed it many times before successfully without paying much attention to the cars going by. So I pushed down on my bike pedal to cross it. As soon as I moved forward only a foot or so my friend, Takayuki, shouted, "Stop!"

It was too late; the momentum carried the bicycle with me toward the middle of the street. I still remember the scene vividly as a slow-motion video. I clearly saw a car coming right at me with a high-pitched braking noise. Believe it or not, I was thinking, "It'll stop just like before." I was overconfident and over-trusting. Suddenly, *bam*, I flew about 10 feet and landed on the top of my head. I was conscious, but I couldn't move my body. Suddenly, I saw many people at the scene and I saw my oldest brother, who happened to be going by on his bicycle, saying to the crowds, "He is my little brother." I was quickly scooped up by the driver and he gently laid me down in the back seat of his car. I heard a woman in the crowd advising the driver to go to the Railroad Hospital, which was one of the closest and oldest general hospitals in Tokyo.

When I arrived at the hospital, a few medical staff members were waiting for me. Probably someone in the crowd had called the hospital as soon as we left the accident scene. I truly appreciated the honest driver and helpful people. Another person in the crowd who knew my family well had run to my mother at work and told her, "Shiro was hit by a car and transported to the Railroad Hospital." Meanwhile, I was quickly laid on a hard stretcher. My head was immobilized with a two-inch-thick rubber band across my forehead, which was anchored on both sides of the stretcher rims. As I was pushed to the emergency room, I noticed how the many ceiling lights flashed with equal distance and time along the long hallway. It was just like a scene from a TV drama.

In the emergency room, the physician quickly performed a thorough physical and mental examination. I had no bleeding and was responsive and appropriate for a seven-year old boy. However, I had a big bump on the top of my head and my left arm and leg were bruised. My head was bandaged in a circular shape from the top of my head, past both ears, and around my chin. My left arm and leg were also bandaged up. Shortly after I was pushed to a spacious recovery room on the same stretcher with a pillow, my mother rushed to me and cried from the top of her lungs, "Shiro, don't die, don't die." She repeated this as she put her face on my chest until my shirt was wet with her tears.

I said to her clearly, so that she could calm herself down, "Mom, I'm not going to die." I wanted to hold her hands but I couldn't move. My body was still in a shock stage. From the time of the accident until I was in the recovery room took less than one hour. I fell asleep and the next thing I remember I was in a nice, comfortable futon in my parents' bedroom, which was right next to the dining room and kitchen, because my mother wanted to keep her eye on me. The accident happened on the first day of spring break. Therefore, my mother wasn't concerned about my missing school, but she informed the school that I was involved in a car accident while riding on a bicycle. Then my first-grade teacher came to see me, and then the assistant principal and principal. Soon we had a lot of baskets of fruits and flowers.

In the middle of this unusual event, the most impressive person except for my mother was the driver. The whole thing had been my fault. I was the one did not pay attention to the traffic. Worse, I was becoming a little impertinent and spoiled; I was completely assuming that all the cars would stop safely whenever I crossed that street. This selfish and irresponsible attitude gave me a good lesson. Despite the fact that the driver had little responsibility for the accident, he came to see me the day after I returned from the hospital and brought a big basket of fruits. He then stayed in touch with my mother daily, either by phone calls or visits, always wearing a suit and tie, until I completely recovered and resumed school. He was a true gentleman. I have a regret that I did not have the courage to thank him for saving my life because he could have run me over and drove away. With the support and love of all the people involved for my recovery, I was able to start the second grade with all my classmates. This was one of the reasons why I was able to maintain a strong drive to accomplish my definite purpose and dreams. I could not disappoint them; I wanted to respond to what they had given me.

In March 1983, I was ready to graduate from Tokyo Bunkyo School for the Blind after completing the Oriental Medicine program. I was looking forward to pursuing something more challenging and stimulating in life. This was my deep-seated desire: to be free from a stereotypical view that visually impaired people must only pursue careers as massage therapists, acupuncturists, or teachers for schools for the blind. I wanted to create a revolution to this stereotyping and I was hoping that one day Japanese society would become tolerant and flexible for all people with disabilities to pursue whatever they wanted. I was determined to prove that those who negatively viewed me or others with disabilities were wrong.

Decision in Oklahoma

I had the fortunate opportunity to join an organization called Friendship Force International, established by a former president of the United States, Jimmy Carter. The concept of this worldwide organization is to achieve world peace by offering ordinary citizens, called "civilian ambassadors," cultural exchange opportunities through two-week home stay experiences in various countries.

I participated in the exchange program by visiting the state of Oklahoma in late April through early May of 1983, which is one of the most beautiful seasons in the South Central region of the United States. After entering the United States through Los Angeles, we flew to Denver, Colorado. Finally, our group of more than 20 people from Japan arrived in Oklahoma City, flying into the Will Rogers Airport at night. All I could see and sense through the huge airport terminal windows was darkness.

My impression of the United States so far was that the interior of the structures was colorful and decorative. For example, the paint on the walls in the Oklahoma City Airport was in primary colors. Along the concourse were paintings of Native Americans, cowboys, and oil fields, which were symbolic of Oklahoma.

By the time we were led to a room full of anticipating host families, who were anxious to meet the guests from the Far East, it had been more than 24 hours since we had left our homes in various areas of Japan. My roommate, Masaki Kanazu, and I were quickly found by our first host family, Howard and Doris Keim. They looked excited about seeing us. They said, "Welcome to Oklahoma," with big smiles, and we all walked to pick up our luggage. Howard and Doris—we called them "Hop and Doris"—were a retired couple. They found significance in the Friendship Force activities by being able to broaden their horizons and contribute to world peace by living and sharing with people from different cultures.

Hop was about six feet, four inches tall, a slender, well-dressed man with a gray sport coat. On the other hand, Doris was about five feet, six inches tall, weighed about 200 pounds, and had a happy, motherly feel. To me, they represented many retired couples in the middle class in that generation.

When we went to the carousel to pick up our luggage, Hop took my heavy suitcase all the way to their Lincoln Town car without rolling it. I was moved that he showed respect for his guest by carrying it more than 200 feet and placing it in the car trunk as gently as possible. I felt that I was learning already how best to treat others.

We all got in the car and headed to Norman, Oklahoma, where they lived. It was dark outside, so I couldn't see any scenery. Although I had been awake more than 25 hours at this time, my adrenaline was working to keep my mind sharp. Honestly, I had been nervous about going abroad for the first time and not being able to understand or speak English. Most of the way to their home, Doris did the speaking. She explained things to us about the state of Oklahoma and what our schedule would be like for the first week with them. She asked Masaki and me questions about our families in Japan. Although I didn't know enough English to respond to her, I noticed that Masaki was nodding and answering her questions. At the time, I had no idea that they were already figuring out who needed more care. That was me.

It took approximately 45 minutes to arrive at Hop and Doris's house. It looked almost exactly like what we had seen in the American movies. Their house was located in a spaciously organized residential area and had a grass front yard and a two-car garage. The entire house resembled a gingerbread house in a children's storybook.

We were then led to the inside of the house. The entrance hall, the spacious living and dining rooms with high ceilings, the oil paintings on the walls, and the decorative items on the coffee table were all purposeful, stylish, and beautiful.

It was already after 10 p.m. We were served glasses of orange juice and led to our bedrooms, which were painted pink and decorated with more beautiful items, such as an antique dresser and a chandelier. We were instructed to sleep in as long as we wanted. Finally, at about midnight, Masaki and I were able to lie down.

I probably slept 10 hours. By the time I sat down at the dining table the next day, it was almost lunch time. On the table sat a business card-sized cowboy belt buckle wrapped in a red, semitransparent paper as a welcoming gift. Doris was explaining something about it, but I couldn't understand what she was saying. I said, "Thank you very much."

The four of us were seated at the table for breakfast at almost at noon. We were served typical southern foods, which were sausages, biscuits, scrambled eggs, and coffee or orange juice. After the meal, Hop said he wanted to take us somewhere. He took us to a shopping mall to buy original cowboy belts with our first names printed on them. When we came back home, Hop showed us how to connect the belt to the buckles so that we could become "Japanese-Oklahomans." I thought these gifts were heartwarming; at the same time, I understood their sense of humor. I wanted to express my sincere appreciation to Hop and Doris. However, I didn't know what to say or how to say it.

Doris began explaining what the schedule looked like for the rest of our first full day. Again, I had no idea what she was letting know us. But Masaki understood English much better than I did. I had started being able to understand "Let's go" and "Come with us" by this time. I tried hard to listen to what everyone was saying and read everyone's movements so that I could compensate for my lack of visual information.

Doris said, "Let's go" that evening, so we all got into the big Lincoln and drove about 10 minutes. We arrived at Hop and Doris's friend's home. Their friend's name was Ernestine Tullius, and she had organized a potluck dinner with many people. To our surprise, one of our ambassadors, Kayoko Saeki, was staying there. Masaki and I were introduced to Ernestine's son, daughter-in-law, neighbors, and their children. They were all so excited about seeing us and to hear that we had traveled halfway around the Earth. Most Oklahomans spend their entire lives without actually meeting a single Japanese person.

After dinner, we showed everyone origami, otedama, kendama, and daruma otoshi, which are traditional Japanese games and toys. They seriously attempted to play with these toys amidst a lot of friendly conversation and laughter. Before we left for the night, many people said they wanted to take us to their homes for horseback riding and country music dance parties. I thought that we had become stars. Though I wasn't able to communicate with them well, I felt that I was somehow touching their hearts.

For the next four days, three Japanese people and their two host families spent most of their activities together. We went to a couple of country dance parties (Oklahomans love country music and dance). Whenever we would go to one of these parties, Doris would ask the band leader to let me play the drums for a song or two. This is because I used to play the drums in a rock and jazz band. Doris created the opportunity for me to express myself and possibly inspire people. I was introduced to probably 100 people with blue jeans, cowboy hats, and boots. I felt their expectations and I was determined that I would not disappoint them, especially Doris. After I played as beautifully as I could, all the band members and Doris and Hop clapped hands. I heard many people saying, "Good job!" and received smiles, shoulder pats, and handshakes from people I did not know. I thought

I might have something that could transcend different people and cultures.

The next day we visited the University of Oklahoma. I was impressed by the size of the campus, which is built like a small town and has facilities such as a hospital, bank, post office, and travel agency—plus a few restaurants and bookstores—in addition to the classroom buildings and sports facilities. We also visited museums like The Cowboy Hall of Fame and The Native American History Museum, had lunch at a Pizza Hut, and traveled to Tulsa in Hop's motorhome, all before the first week of the cultural exchange programs had ended.

Masaki, who was an architect and who had graduated from one of the best universities in Japan—Kyoto University—complimented me, saying, "Shiro, you are amazing!" Kayoko, too, praised how I touched people's hearts and souls, even with little ability to communicate in English. These two Japanese people were seriously praising and acknowledging my special abilities to move people. I felt that I had finally achieved a certain confidence, which enabled me to create the ending scene of a movie in my mind, one in which I wore a cap and gown, and attended a college commencement ceremony in the United States.

The night before we left the host family's house, I started seriously preparing to ask the most important question in my life. I wanted to ask Doris her honest opinion about whether I could study physical therapy (PT) in the United States. I probably spent an hour looking up words in the dictionary with my magnifying lenses to compose a perfect question so that I could seek her honest opinion about my intention.

On our last morning with Doris and Hop, Doris knocked on my bedroom door as usual and kindly said, "Shiro, it's morning." It was a crisp and beautiful Oklahoma morning in late April. When I came out of the bedroom, I smelled coffee, sausage, and biscuits. Doris wore a pretty pink house coat while sitting in her reclining chair, reading a magazine. Hop had on brown trousers with a white dress shirt, reading a newspaper in his recliner. My roommate was sitting on a couch. I guessed everyone was waiting for me to have our last breakfast together before Masaki and I went to our second host families separately.

After having a friendly breakfast, I cleaned the bedroom that I had slept in for a week. There was still one hour or so before Doris and Hop would drive me to a location in Oklahoma City to meet my second host family. I sat on a couch in the living room with the clear intention of asking my question of Doris. I had complete respect for her honest opinions. She changed into her dress and came into the living room to sit in her recliner chair. She relaxed by putting her legs on the leg rest.

The perfect timing! I thought. Then I asked Doris a few English sentences, which I had practiced many times in my mind since the night before.

"Doris," I said, gaining her attention.

"Yes, Shiro?" she responded. At this moment she sensed something important coming.

I asked with a straight face, "May I ask you a question?"

"Yes, you may," she replied.

"Do you think I can study physical therapy in the United States?"

She answered with confidence, "Sure, you can," as if she was saying that it shouldn't be a problem with my intelligence and personality. As soon as she said that, I gave myself a "GO" sign to carry out this big plan. No one but Doris, Hop, and my mother believed that I would earn an American college degree and become a physical therapist in the United States. This was the biggest idea for the ending scene of my autobiographical movie in my imagination at that time.

In summary: I participated in the cultural exchange program in Oklahoma because I wanted to feel out how I engaged with people and how I would be received by them. I asked Doris about my desire to attend a college and become a physical therapist in the United States. Her confident "Sure, you can," inspired me to take action toward my definite purpose.

Find Your Definite Purpose

Ask yourself:

- What is the most ideal life for me?
- What do I really enjoy doing?
- When do I truly feel good about myself?

Then choose one possibility that would provide you with your most fulfilling life and that would help elevate the lives of others.

It is absolutely important that you find your purpose by being fully committed to knowing where you are going and what you want in life. The purpose has to be definite and you need to create a picture in your mind of you already achieving your goal. All the greatest inventions—automobiles, airplanes, computers, smart phones, renewable energy devices, various technologies based on AI, new types of vaccines, and everything else—were started with imagination. Use the power of your mind to imagine your bright future. Can you visualize the ending scene of your own heroic movie? Yes, you can. Let your desire drive you all the way to your dream.

See the "Exercises for Your Dream" section for steps on how you can develop and identify your own definite purpose.

Chapter 2

DESIRE—
The Driving Force Moving You to Attain Your Definite Purpose

When desire becomes burning desire, all you need is a one-way-ticket to your ideal destination. You must be willing to overcome many challenges to attain your most precious human desire, and to achieve independence and ultimate freedom.

A year and a half after my visit to Oklahoma, I found myself on a 10-and-a-half-hour flight on a Northwest Boeing 747 from Tokyo to the Los Angeles International Airport. I hardly remember what I was doing or thinking on this flight. This was probably because I was very nervous about what I hoped would be a smooth entry into the United States, and about catching my two connecting flights in a timely manner to my final destination of Lawrence, Kansas, where the University of Kansas (KU) is located. I also had no idea how long it would take to be accepted into a state physical therapy school.

In the midst of all these worries, I was determined not to return home to see my family until I had received an acceptance letter from my chosen physical therapy school in a warm climate. But I do remember that one thing I did again and again on the airplane was to listen to Tatsuro Yamashita's *Big Wave* soundtrack album on my Walkman. His songs allowed me to feel free from any self-imposed limitations or social conformities, which are cultural characteristics of Japanese society.

In the early '80s, the jetways that connected airplanes to airport terminals were not often available. Consequently, we all stepped down a set of stairs to the tarmac and were guided to immigration clearance. As I stepped out of the airplane and came down the steps, I still vividly remember the feeling of the West Coast—the crisp and fresh air that wrapped around me and the clearest, bluest sky I had ever seen in my entire life. It was such a monumental moment for me to be free from the past and to begin walking toward my second life in the United States.

There were five or six windows to line up at for the immigration clearance. I simply stood in the line closest to me because all the lines were the same length and the space was crowded. The line seemed to be moving quickly, and when my turn came I handed over my documents, including my passport and the I–20, proving that I had been accepted by the Applied English Center at the University of Kansas. The immigration officer examining my documents asked me something, but I did not understand a word of English. At the same time, I did not know what to say to him. Being able to say, "I beg your pardon?" or "Would you please repeat it again?" was months or a year ahead of me at that time. Unfortunately, I also could not identify where he was looking and I wasn't able to make eye contact with him either. So he asked an assistant who understood Japanese; she told me to step aside and wait until they completed processing all the other passengers on the flight.

All the passengers except me were processed about an hour later. I found myself sitting alone on a typical airport seat in the back of the immigration processing area. I was anxious about whether or not I could enter the United States, but I believed that I had brought and presented the right documents. Another hour passed by. At this point, my major concern was whether or not I could catch my first connecting flight to Kansas City. Finally, the Japanese assistant walked toward me holding my documents. I sensed that I was able to move on because of the way she walked toward me. She said, "Okay, Mr. Iwae, let's get your new connecting flights first because you already missed your original flights." It had been about two hours since I was told to "step aside and wait." Nevertheless, I was so happy that I could start out for my second life from sunny Southern California.

She quickly brought me my suitcase, then we went to the Northwest Airlines information booth to find the next flight to Kansas City. I thought of how my second life had already begun with thrill and adventure. First, I missed all the connecting flights and I had no idea how to contact the Foreign Students Office of the university to reach out to the secretary who was scheduled to pick me up today at the Lawrence Regional Airport. I was supposed to have had a smooth entry to the university within 24 hours of leaving

Tokyo. Instead, my next flight to Kansas City would leave at midnight for Philadelphia, arriving about eight the next morning, and reconnecting to Kansas City at 9:45 a.m. In any case, I would safely make entry into the United States. I expressed my sincere appreciation to this woman for assisting me in making a good start toward reaching my dream.

100 Percent Responsible

After I checked my luggage, I was very hungry and I felt a little cold, because the airport building was well air conditioned. First I went to a gift shop to look for a sweatshirt to keep myself warm. Even though it was August, I instinctively knew that I had to prepare for another 24-hour trip to my final destination. So I purchased a white sweatshirt with a hood that had "California" written in sky blue on the left chest. Then I went to find something to eat to keep my energy and spirit up. In 1984, it was common to carry traveler's checks for international travels because they were guaranteed to be replaced in case they were lost or stolen. I used a traveler's check to pay for my sweatshirt and food, feeling the beginnings of a good sense of independence.

From now on, I would be responsible for all the decisions that I made.

I hardly remember how I spent the seven or eight hours in the airport until boarding the midnight flight to Philadelphia. Nonetheless, it was not boring; I was so fascinated observing people with such a wide range of nationalities, ages, fashion, body types, and spoken languages. I came to the awareness that the United States was a small version of the world. I felt that these people were exuding intentional and purposeful energy to reach their destinations and achieve something in their lives. Although I didn't know how long it would take to actualize my desire to become a physical therapist here in the land of opportunities, I believed what all the people I truly respected said about my potential, abilities, and personality. It became my habit to keep reminding myself, "Yes, I can."

After having a late-night dinner, I walked to the gate for the flight to Philadelphia. All I needed to do on the flight was to have a good night's sleep for the next day. I fell asleep as soon as I fastened my seatbelt for takeoff and I slept most of the way there. When I walked out to the gate and the waiting area, no one was around; it was too early in the morning for travelers to wait for departing flights. I quickly checked the gate for my Kansas City flight so that I felt secure in resting two more hours on an airport seat to save my physical and mental energy for any unexpected happenings. I was already learning how to protect and prepare myself for living in the United States for years to come.

In those days, a complete airline breakfast was often served on planes, with ceramic plates and metal forks and knives, even in economy class. I really looked forward to having such a meal on the airplane because it was something special to be served while in the sky, above the clouds. About three hours later, I arrived at the Kansas City Airport. When I stepped into the airport arrival gate, I immediately felt welcomed by the bright, warm-colored wooden floor and the abundance of natural light. To my surprise, my Lawrence flight was right next to the gate where I arrived from Philadelphia.

Before I approached the attendant to show him my ticket to Lawrence, Kansas, I composed in my mind the best sentence possible to convey what I wanted to do. I walked up to the gentleman with all my enthusiasm and showed him the ticket. Before I could take a deep breath to speak to him, he gave me a friendly smile and said, "Are you Mr. Shiro Iwae? Is this your luggage?" After all that practicing, my words went unused. All I needed to say was "Yes, thank you." I was so happy to find that my luggage from halfway around the world was right next to me and that they would take me to Lawrence.

When I was ticketed, he said, "We will depart in 30 minutes or so."

I replied, "Okay, thank you." I had no idea how far Lawrence was from the Kansas City Airport, but I was expecting another short jet plane flight.

A little while later, the gentleman who had taken care of me so far said, "Are you ready to go?"

I said, "Yes."

Then he picked up my heavy suitcase, guided me to the stairs that went down to the tarmac, and led me to a single-engine Cessna. He put my luggage in the small cargo space and opened the backseat door for me to be seated on the plane.

Some people would be scared of riding in such a small aircraft. However, I looked forward to experiencing seeing the landscape from 3,000 feet above the earth. I buckled my seatbelt; I was ready for takeoff.

The man climbed into the cockpit and started communicating with the air traffic controller for permission to taxi the plane toward the runway. As soon as the plane came to a stop at the end of it, this pilot—who did everything else too—said to me, "We will take off." I couldn't respond with voice; I just nodded. I had finally become nervous about flying in this small airplane, but there was no way of stopping or going back. It was already accelerating down the runway. I closed my eyes for a moment and it quickly took off. I felt that I was gently pushed up by the floor of the plane as we climbed up into the air of the Midwest blue sky.

The view from the window was of light green grasses along with deep green forest. It looked like the opening scene of *The Sound of Music*, where it showed the beautiful rolling hills. Although it was a less than a 30-minute flight altogether, I was fascinated by the magnificent scenery, including the far distant horizon. The airplane smoothly descended and landed in the Lawrence Regional Airport. It taxied toward a small structure that looked like a wooden house and stopped about 100 feet in front of it. The pilot stepped off the plane and opened my door. He let me know that we had arrived in Lawrence and that he would bring my suitcase to the check-in luggage spot.

I put my backpack on my back and started walking toward the small airport terminal when I noticed a woman standing beside the entrance. As I came closer she asked, "Are you Shiro?"

I responded, "Yes."

"I am Kathy from the University of Kansas. I am here to pick you up."

I was so pleased to know that I was finally able to reach the university after more than 48 hours of traveling from Tokyo. I noticed I was finally able to let my tensed-up nerves relax a little because I felt that someone was on my side and I was not alone. I picked up my luggage and followed her to the parking lot.

She said, "Here is my car." It was a big blue American convertible. She opened the trunk for me to place my belongings inside, then said, "Okay, let's go."

It was my first ride in a big convertible. She started driving the straight country road between grass fields with the summer sun above us, the wind blowing her blonde hair and filling our ears with noise. Since I'd met her, I'd been wondering how she was able to come to the airport to pick me up in spite of my day's delay. I began composing a question in my head to ask her, "Why were you able to know what day and time I would arrive in Lawrence?" However, I just did not have enough energy or confidence to communicate with her in the overwhelming wind and its noise. So I leaned back against my seat and put my wonder away.

Exchange Student, Hironobu Takada

After an exhausting trip, I finally arrived at the Foreign Students Office on the campus. As soon as I stepped into the poorly lit wooden interior, which was the size of an average child's bedroom, I was asked to fill out forms with basic information about myself to register my official entry into the United States and the university. However, I could not understand a word of English that the director of the office, Dr. Clark, said to me. At the same time, I had neither the skills nor energy to say, "I beg your pardon?" or "Would you please explain it slowly?" So I was silent and just stared at the form to pretend that I could read the printed words without giant magnification. The secretary who picked me up from the airport noticed that I needed help to fill it out, so she asked another Japanese student who happened to be there to assist me in completing the registration.

He approached me rather carefully, as most Japanese people do when meeting someone for the first time. He introduced himself, saying in English, "My name is Hironobu Takada; it's nice to meet you." I did not know how to react to another Japanese person speaking to me in English. But I quickly realized that it was proper manners to use English as a common language when non-Japanese speakers were around.

In any case, I was mentally and physically too exhausted to deal with another word of English, so I used a quiet voice to introduce my name and asked him, "What do I need to write down on this application?" He pointed to where I needed to fill things in, but I couldn't see what he was pointing out. I had to tell him, "I am legally blind. Would you fill in all the spaces on the paper?"

He said "OK," and eventually, I was able to complete the registration for my initial entry into the university through the Foreign Students Office. After that, I found that Hironobu was to be my roommate in temporary housing until the campus dormitories opened for the very first fall semester of my American college experience in 1984.

Hironobu was a senior exchange student from Tsukuba University, which is one of the well-known national universities in Japan. Meeting him was impactful on my academic success in years to come. I had not met such a person who clearly told me with confidence that his life's purpose was to go to a good college, including studying abroad, and succeed in the corporate world in Japan. He even told me that he would climb up the corporate ladder to succeed in the Mitsubishi Bank, which was one of the largest banks in Japan at that time and still is. He proudly claimed that he was not interested in anything other than a 4.0 GPA in his academic career, including here at the University of Kansas. He even had a concrete image of what type of woman he would be married to and in what kind of house he wanted to live. I was amazed at such an individual whose priorities were extremely focused on personal achievements and success in life. I thought that someone like him only existed in books or movies. He was not the typical student who was just hungry for excellent grades and future corporate success. This was why it was a positive and transformative experience for me to be acquainted with him.

Hironobu had friendly smiles, a good sense of humor, and a variety of interests in the world. For instance, one day after school I said to him, "I need to buy a soap because it is becoming small."

He philosophically replied, "The soap will start lasting long when it gets small."

This was his thoughtful way of telling me, "Don't worry, I'll go to the store with you later this week." Decades later, I still remember the truth in his clever response whenever I see a small soap that's been used for a few weeks.

He once asked me to go see a movie downtown. The movie was called *Ten*, which referred to the highest score a beautiful a woman could achieve. We were the only people in the movie theater in the middle of the day. We enjoyed the movie and each other's company, and we discussed girls and women as we rode the campus bus all the way back to our dormitory.

I learned a huge difference in Hironobu's study habits compared with mine. He spent more time pursuing the depths of what he was trying to study and what it meant for practical applications to real life. On the contrary, I had never developed such an attitude toward learning because

I had not been allowed to apply myself so competitively. Furthermore, I was not interested in understanding the power of knowledge or how to excel in school until I met him.

Thus, getting to know and be influenced by him gave me one of the greatest gifts to launch my new academic career and bright future. For example, he used the library as much as possible because it provided not only a quiet, spacious, and comfortable environment in which to concentrate, but also because of the assistance of the librarians between 7 o'clock in the morning until 10 o'clock at night. He always knew and organized his priorities as if he had already imagined his own autobiographical movie. Later, I found that this was what Napoleon Hill described in his well-known book *Think and Grow Rich*. Hill observed and studied more than 500 highly successful people to reveal why they were successful. I was very fortunate to meet Hironobu at the beginning of creating my second life in the United States.

Freedom to Learn

I exploded as if was a rocket carrying astronauts to the International Space Station. For a long time, I had felt that I was prohibited from trying to see how much I could academically excel. Because of my visual impairment, I was almost always treated as a pupil who was in a specially protected category for all six years of regular elementary school. Then, when I began going to the school for the blind, which was from middle school through acupuncture school—nine years of education— I felt that I was in a comfortably heated pool of low expectation.

After I felt free to learn and test my ability wholeheartedly, I was ready to start from zero. In other words, I was so ready to repaint myself on a clean white canvas. On the very first day of my KU student life, I went to the Applied English Center (AEC) to inform them that I had safely arrived at KU and to register to take the Michigan English Test. This test was for examining English proficiency to classify newly arriving international students into appropriate class levels.

Since the university had opened in 1866, many buildings on campus were made of stone and wood. Lippincott Hall housed the AEC, and was one of oldest structures. I pulled open one side of the tall and heavy wooden double-entrance doors. On both sides of the entrance hall were two wooden staircases that led to one large landing. From there, wide stairs led to the AEC on the second floor. These steps were not perfectly flat and made squeaky noises as I climbed up. It reminded me of the old church that I used to go to when I was in elementary school in Tokyo.

The AEC office looked like a gymnasium capable of hosting a basketball game. I saw a few international students chatting in English and sometimes in their mother languages. *Wow,* I thought, *I am no longer in a highly segregated and protected school for the blind,* which I had been in from middle school until finishing acupuncture school in Japan. I was committed to sail in a big ocean. I reminded myself that there would be serious years ahead of me and many difficulties to overcome. I encouraged myself to endure anything and achieve my dream no matter what. I was so happy to be free to have this incredible opportunity of learning and studying as hard as I could.

I repeated a few lines in my head while I stood in front of the receptionist who displayed a gentle and respectful manner toward new students. My turn came and I stepped up to the reception counter. I said, "Hi, my name is Shiro Iwae and I safely arrived."

She gave me a big smile and said, "Welcome to the University of Kansas."

This was only the fourth day into my American college life. However, I definitely felt that the American people were generous and proud of being American. They also loved their home state. I took care of all the necessary paperwork and registration for the Michigan Test.

I was nervous about how long it would take to earn an American college degree in physical therapy. However, my burning desire to prove that I was capable of receiving the degree was so overwhelmingly powerful that nervousness became a negligible natter.

On the day of the Michigan Test, I was in a huge auditorium. About 100 international students from all over the world were seated two seats apart to preventing cheating. This did not matter to me because my visual acuity was 20/200. I knew that I would begin with the lowest level of language proficiency in the English program. I had to use my handheld magnifying lenses to take this extensive test with normally sighted students. In addition, I had never taken a mark sheet test in my entire life. As a result, I was assigned to the most basic level of English proficiency. This meant that I had to clear five more levels, excluding the current Level I. I totally accepted the result and I was happy to begin with a fresh start, as if I had become a 24-year-old first grader. I looked forward to building a great foundation for my academic career and enduring benefits in the future.

I began taking all basic levels of classes, such as reading comprehension, grammar, listening and speaking, and writing. Most of the teachers were graduate students majoring in linguistics. They were very friendly, thoughtful, and encouraging. In the first or second class meeting, the teachers noticed that I was using the magnifying lenses to look at the text books. I was reading them as if my nose were sweeping ink on the pages. Moreover, I was the slowest student to read, turn the pages, and react to the teachers' instructions because of my visual impairment.

One day, my reading teacher suggested something that would help. "Shiro, there is an office that assists students with temporary or permanent disabilities. I am pretty sure that they will help you to achieve your academic goals," he said with a smile.

Fairness, Equal Opportunities, and Hope

That afternoon I visited the Student Assistance Center to make an appointment for a consultation. The secretary took my name and noted my type of disability. She told me kindly, "Dr. Henderson is available tomorrow at 11:30. Are you available?"

Here came the most convenient reply word in the English language: "Sure," I responded.

"I'll pencil it down." she said. I had no idea what she meant. All I understood was to come back tomorrow at 11:25 to see the counselor.

The next day I was led to the Dr. Henderson's office. When the door was opened, she stood up and said, "Welcome to the University of Kansas. I'm very pleased to meet you." She smiled and shook my hand. She was tall, with short, curly blonde hair and dangling earrings. After we sat down, she asked, "How may I help you?"

I began explaining my visual impairment and I stated my desire to successfully become a physical therapist in the United States. "How wonderful it is!" she said. She displayed excitement because she knew that people with disabilities seldom set a goal so high. She mentioned that I was entitled to be accommodated with readers, note takers, extra time for tests, recording assistance, magnification in prints or use of a magnifying device, and an isolated testing environment. I was impressed that such a system was in place for people with disabilities to help them be as independent and successful as possible. She carefully and slowly asked me, "What types of assistance do you think you need?"

"I need a note taker and extra time for testing, use of a magnifying device, and an isolated testing room," I said.

She said, "You've got it," and smiled as if she wanted to give me a high five. At the end of our conversation she sincerely and firmly said, "You may see me any time you want." As I left the office, I felt my hope to be able to earn my first American college degree grow.

By the next day, all of my teachers had received a letter from Dr. Henderson requesting appropriate accommodations for my classroom activities and testing. With this system in place, I quickly became one of the top students in each class. Moreover, my positive and sincere attitude toward learning was respected by my teachers as well as my classmates. I showed up to all of my classes on time and turned in homework promptly with neat handwriting.

At the end of the first semester, all the AEC students took the Michigan Test to determine whether or not they would progress to a higher level. I also took the test. This time, I understood that I was entitled to request the testing arrangements that best suited me. I was placed with a proctor in a room in the main library that housed a magnifying reading monitor. I was allowed 100 percent extended time and was told to simply circle the right answers on the test; then the proctor would transcribe the answers onto a mark sheet. Because of my diligent work, I was able to advance to Level II in the spring semester of 1985.

Commencement Ceremony

In May of 1985, Hironobu asked me to go with him to see a graduation ceremony at the KU football stadium. We were eager to experience American culture and we had a longing to wear the cap and gown that would proudly show our academic achievement. I believed that most of the serious international students were picturing themselves wearing that regalia and receiving their diploma showing an American college degree was awarded. The ceremony was known to be very special.

It was a beautiful spring weekend. We saw many well-dressed family members of the thousands of graduates walking toward the main entrance gate. We climbed up the stairs at about the 50-yard line and looked down at the well-kept green turf. It was our first time viewing such a beautifully designed stadium and attending an American college commencement. We were stimulated and inspired by the well-organized ceremony, the KU president's speech, the "Pomp and Circumstance March" performed by the KU orchestra, and the smiles, cheers, clapping, tears, and other types of joyous expressions. I didn't know when it would happen, but I was inspired that someday I would be in that special seat with the cap and gown.

During the summer semester I progressed to the Level III language proficiency, and I began with Level IV in fall 1985. I kept improving my English proficiency each semester. Furthermore, by the end of that summer I no longer had to take the reading comprehension or the listening and speaking classes. Since US immigration law requires all international students to maintain at least 12 credit hours per semester, I added a swimming class and an intermediate mathematics course in place of the AEC English grammar and writing classes. During transition from the AEC to the regular university courses, most undergraduate advisors recommended that international students in general take mathematics. This was because math courses do not involve much reading and writing. In addition, mathematics was, in a way, a universal language. My math course became a smooth transition tool for me prior to taking the undergraduate courses that would require a lot of reading and writing, such as English, psychology, sociology, and humanities.

Scholarships

By the end of fall 1985, I had earned straight As in the four consecutive semesters since I had arrived at KU. Now I felt that I had some actual achievements to apply for as many scholarships as I wanted. So I asked Dr. Henderson at the Student Assistance Center about scholarships for which I could apply. She showed me two types of scholarships. One was a $500 tuition scholarship and another was a bookstore scholarship. I asked her, "Could I apply for both?"

She smiled and replied, "Of course!"

So I prepared an honest and passionate essay for those two scholarships. I thought that this was a great opportunity to not only improve my writing skills but also demonstrate my potential to contribute to society.

Several weeks later, I received a couple of letters from those scholarship sponsors. I neatly cut open the side of the first envelope with scissors in case I wanted to frame the letter later. I pulled out the letter slowly, hoping for good news. I opened the letter and picked up a magnifying lens to read it. I read the very first line, stating, "Congratulations!"

"Great!" I said.

Then I read the rest of the letter; it was the $500 tuition scholarship. I opened the second envelope in the same manner and found the same statement, "Congratulations!"

I thought how generous the United States was to give such rewards to an unknown international student who showed only four semesters of academic results in courses that were mostly not even regular university courses. Furthermore, the quality of my essay might have only been that of an average American seventh-grade student. Since then, whenever I was asked about my impression of the United States, either by Americans or Japanese, I always answered, "This country has an incredible capacity to be generous to people with good intention." After such a touching experience, I studied even more diligently because I did not want to disappoint those who gave me such recognition.

In my fifth semester, all I had left was a special writing course that did not meet in the classroom. It was an independent study course for which I went to the AEC office and picked up a weekly writing assignment. I turned in the best possible writing I could in terms of content as well as quality, always with neat handwriting. The instructor recorded her feedback on a cassette tape. I always enjoyed listening to her comments because her voice was gentle and her feedback was positive and encouraging. While I was taking this last AEC course, I was also taking an algebra/trigonometry course and a swimming course to maintain the 12 credit hours per semester. So I completed the spring of 1986 with straight As, and fortunately my tuition and books were paid for by the scholarships. I thanked all the people who believed in me, including my mother, Hop and Doris, Dr. Henderson, and all the AEC teachers. Within five semesters, I had completed the intensive English program. I felt a strong sense of confidence that I had attained a good foundation to start taking prerequisite courses for admission to a chosen physical therapy school.

In summary: At the University of Kansas, I built a foundation of the English language. At the same time, I gained hope for a bright future by meeting mindful and intellectual people who gave me the positive affirmation and conviction to pursue my ambitious academic goals and dreams.

Recognize Your Desire

Ask yourself, *What do I really want to change, demonstrate, respond to, or prove in the world in which I live?* You must have something deep inside of your heart and mind.

Desire is a highly emotionalized source of power, like an engine in a car. It drives you all the way to attain your definite purpose. Your burning desire allows you to develop resourcefulness, self-initiative, self-reliance, imagination, faith, a cooperative spirit, and a positive attitude, which attracts people to help you reach your dream. For instance, my driving power originated when I responded to the unconditional love that my mother and grandmother gave me. Can you find the source of a highly emotional driving force from your past, your present experiences, or your future concerns? Yes, you can. Use it to empower you to achieve your major purpose and to make yourself useful in the world.

"Exercises for Your Dream" will show you how you can recognize and harness the power you have in your heart.

Chapter 3

ORGANIZED PLANNING—Establishing Strategies, Assembling Alliances, and Going the Extra Mile

Your success consists of many factors, including luck and coincidence. However, it will be extremely difficult to achieve without well-thought-out strategies and genuine interest in people.

I transferred to Northern Arizona University (NAU) in Flagstaff in the fall of 1986. This was because I wanted to see other parts of the country while steadily completing as many prerequisite courses as possible to apply for a physical therapy school in Florida. By this time, I started understanding the serious nature of being one of 30 to 35 physical therapy students (out of 600 to 700 candidates) chosen to attend a state school. Those who pursued this major had to demonstrate academic excellence at the very least. However, I knew that physical therapy schools did not choose students based on their academic performances alone. My life's philosophy is to apply myself to be the best I can; every experience nurtures the process of my growth as a sensible and worldly human being.

I knew that I must keep my grade point average at 3.75 or above in order to be selected by any PT schools in the nation. Thus, I spoke to the coordinator, Ms. Jane Mooruney, at the Office of Students with Disabilities about whether or not I could take 10 credit hours per regular semester instead of 12 credit hours. This idea turned into a small negotiation with the US Citizenship and Immigration Services because I was requesting an exception to the rule that all undergraduate students must maintain at least 12 hours of course work per semester.

Jane understood that I could not afford to earn even a B, especially in science courses. So she spoke with the director at the International Students Office to inquire if I could be exempted from the rule. The director said to Jane, "Yes, he may go with a slower pace." Later, Jane called to tell me the news on our dormitory room's push-button phone. (In 1986, we didn't even have email, and cellular phone availability was well beyond a decade into the future. I used to write many letters to my mother and friends. It was such an era.)

Taking prerequisites at a slower pace meant that I had to exercise tremendous discipline because other students were able to take pre-physical therapy courses much faster than me. Taking more time to complete my courses meant that I needed more money to live on. In other words, I was delaying becoming a physical therapist and earning an income so that I could be a truly independent adult. Therefore, I was absolutely determined to obtain any type of scholarship that I could.

Decision

For science prerequisites, I had to take two semesters of biology, chemistry, and physics, including laboratory classes. Since I had studied anatomy and physiology in Japan, I took BIO 201 Anatomy and Physiology with a lab, in addition to intermediate English and an Enjoyment of Music class. I knew that I would be able to earn As in those courses. However, the anatomy and physiology course was questionable because of the many technical terms that had to be thoroughly understood.

In the first lecture of Anatomy and Physiology, I felt that two years of English proficiency preparation might not be good enough for an A in a critical course like this. This was because the professor, Dr. David Markle, didn't design the course for an international student like me. The level of the course was geared toward those who were aiming to major in various medical fields, such as medicine, nursing, physical therapy, and so forth. Hence, the lectures moved fast and included many unfamiliar technical terms that originated in Latin and Greek. In addition, the textbook was thick and heavy—about 1,000 pages long.

At the end of the first lecture, Dr. Markle made an announcement to the class explaining my circumstances and stating that I needed a volunteer note taker in this class. When he announced this to the more than 100 students, my heart started racing and my body began warming up. I was nervous about how the students might respond. What if no one wanted to be my note taker? They say that 99 percent of worries are never realized. That is exactly what happened. As soon as the announcement ended, approximately 10 students surrounded Dr. Markle to express their willingness to become a volunteer note taker for me. Suddenly my pulse rate went back down to normal. I felt so appreciative that so many people wanted to help me. Dr. Markle quickly realized that It would be difficult for me to decide who would be the most appropriate helper for someone like me. I ended up having two female classmates, because if one was absent from a lecture, I could rely on the other. The note taking system was quite simple: I supplied a note pad with a carbon sheet. During the lecture, the student took notes as she usually did. Then she gave me the face page and she kept the carbon copy. This analog method would continue until I earned my first bachelor's degree in physical therapy in 1993.

Despite my two very friendly and reliable note takers, the professor often asked me how well I was following the lectures. I had a gut feeling that I had to drop the course in order to avoid earning less than an A grade. After I took the first quiz about three weeks into the semester, I decided to drop it. Dr. Markle agreed with my decision. However, I asked him if I could keep attending the class even without the grade and credits. He said, "Yes, absolutely," with a friendly smile. I finished that fall semester with two neatly handwritten sets of notes from Anatomy and Physiology 201. Because of this rare effort, which very few people did, I was able to earn a B in Anatomy and Physiology 202 and an A for its lab the following spring semester of 1987.

After I finished the first academic year at NAU, I continued to take summer courses. Since all the dormitories closed between semesters for cleaning and system maintenance, most international students had to find a place to stay for a couple of weeks. Even though I had managed to receive some type of scholarship every academic year, I had to be frugal and about how I used money because I did not know when I would become a physical therapist and start making a living on my own. So I put my information-gathering antenna up to find a way to live on campus and possibly earn some money. I heard that the job of dorm cleaning would allow me to stay on campus free of charge while I earned a minimum wage. I immediately contacted the university's custodial services about whether or not they were recruiting people for the job. I was lucky;

the job was available. I was given temporary housing at no cost and I could earn a few hundred dollars while I was employed by them. It felt great that I was stepping toward another independent phase in my life. I felt good about myself for making honest money and being able to deposit it into my bank account.

I then moved to a dorm for summer school. Since not many people took summer school, only one dormitory was open for NAU students. When I look back now, I marvel at how easily I did these frequent moves so many times by walking up and down the huge campus about a quarter to a third of a mile. In addition, I walked to classes all day long, then returned to the dorm to eat and study more every day. I also still had plenty of energy to study at the library on the weekends. Furthermore, I socialized with many students and people in the community, both on and off campus. I now recognize that this was a true sign of youthfulness. I was able to freely explore my maximal abilities in every direction. I innocently had confidence in myself and a picture in my mind of being admitted to my chosen physical therapy school.

The Roommate

I received my key and entered the room with my suitcase and backpack. As I was putting my belongings away in the closet and organizing around my desk, my roommate for the summer semester entered the room. He appeared well-dressed, as he had just returned from traveling and was refreshed. I introduced myself and walked toward him to shake his hand. "Hi, I'm Shiro. Nice meeting you," I said.

He smiled and responded the same way. "I'm Winson. Nice meeting you too." Then I found that he was from Hong Kong and had visited friends in Canada before starting his academic career, majoring in electrical engineering.

We were both freshmen; therefore, we could not yet officially declare a major. A major could be truly determined only after you completed prerequisites with certain grades to be admitted to a department in a field of study. Some people took only two years to satisfy the prerequisites. However, I took six years getting ready for my chosen physical therapy program.

Winson and I were both Asian and intended to be in serious majors. I felt that he would be a positive influence on me to keep up my high academic performances. I was impressed by his unshakable determination to make a living as an electrical engineer in the United States. The next day, many more students came to our dorm for summer school. One of them was my roommate's high school friend, Rosanna, who came to our room to see him. After a brief conversation between them in Cantonese, he introduced her to me with the usual "Nice meeting you" greeting. I asked her, "What are you going to major in?"

She smiled and proudly answered, "I am going to study physical therapy."

I was so happy to hear that another international student expressed this same purpose with conviction. I felt that I might have a good summer knowing these two people who were absolutely committed to create their futures.

We three young students were aiming for nothing but As in all our courses to achieve the lives we dreamed of. One of the most impressive things about Winson and Rosanna was that they had absolutely clear purposes of why they were there. At the same time, they were well-balanced students. For example, my roommate enjoyed dining. He loved the foods he grew up eating in Hong Kong. Therefore, he usually prepared his own meals in our dormitory room using his hotplate and rice cooker. Then he ate it with the happiest face I had ever seen in my life. These meals were simple, such as a little softly cooked rice and a piece of meat with some seasoning. He was willing to spend time and energy for this enriching and relaxing part of his day. He also enjoyed classical music, especially a violin sonata or concerto. He put significant value on his friendship with Rosanna. They usually got together to cook something a little more elaborate by reserving the dormitory kitchen on Friday or Saturday nights. I had a gut feeling that what they had was just what I needed to learn to enhance my American experiences in years to come.

It took a good month or more for Winson and I to finally become more than just roommates. In other words, we reached a certain point of respect and trust in each other. The first sign of that acceptance was when he offered me a piece of well-done meat during lunchtime in our room. He said, "Shiro, would you like to try some meat?" I was so happy that he finally asked me about the meat because of the way he enjoyed the food, almost any food, and ate it as if he was in heaven. He was very proud of his cooking methods, which he based upon physical and chemical sciences. I complimented him on how delicious the meat was and expressed my sincere appreciation for his generosity and opening his heart to me. This moment was the beginning of our lasting friendship.

Summer school was known to be very intense because the same amount of course contents had to be learned in about half the time of regular semesters. Both Rosanna and my roommate were good at math and sciences (Asian people were thought to be generally good at those subjects during '80s). Moreover, since they grew up in Hong Kong, which was under the rule of Great Britain, they were familiar with learning things in English. As a result, their transition to American college education from the first semester was relatively smooth. They possessed a solid foundation of how to learn and compete.

On the contrary, this was the ninth semester for me. I still struggled with how to learn effectively and compete, probably because I had not been expected to excel academically throughout my education in Japan. People with disabilities were unfortunately classified as minor league players in Japanese society. Consequently, I did not develop a solid educational foundation.

When I observed how Rosanna and Winson applied themselves to their American college education, I recognized that I would need to overcome countless hurdles just to get to the point of applying for physical therapy school. Despite these obvious obstacles, I still felt optimistic toward my future.

Driver's License

My two new friends earned straight As. On the other hand, I had to drop my first semester Inorganic Chemistry class. The reason was the same as when I dropped Human Anatomy and Physiology. But I kept attending the class for my future attempt. Once again, the dormitory was closing for fall semester. Winson and I were roommates again between the summer and fall semesters and worked to clean the dormitories six hours a day for two weeks; it was a messy, filthy, and dusty job. However, we accepted and understood it as a fair trade-off. We considered this a very minor inconvenience compared with what we were pursuing for our futures.

After having dinner with me in our room one evening, Winson asked for my opinion and help. "Shiro, I really want to get a driver's license," he said. "But no one will let me borrow a car to do driving practice."

He continued to explain. "This is what I think; I want to buy a nice used car so that I can practice driving all I want, any time I want. Is there any way that you can lend me $500?"

I responded with enthusiasm. "Sure, let's do it, Winson."

I totally understood his frustration that it was inconvenient not being able to drive when he was completely capable of driving. I remembered that I used to walk at least 40 minutes one way to the nearest oriental grocery store when I was in Kansas. In addition, I had to cross an eight-lane road. Because I couldn't see the traffic lights, I used to take time to carefully observe how the cars flowed in this big intersection. I learned to utilize the cars as traffic lights so that I could safely cross almost any road in the United States. I was a tortoise; but I believed that there were 101 ways to get things done, including my dream.

In 1987, various cars were sold for less than $1,000. So we were optimistic that we could buy one for $500 or less. We made an appointment to see a car owner who owned a red two-door 1984 Nissan Centra. We met him in a parking lot on campus, which was almost empty because it was between semesters. We shook hands and he showed us the car. I sensed that he was very motivated to sell it because of his body language, and his polite and honest descriptions of it. He said, "I will give you a ride so that you will feel how good the car runs."

Winson asked him probably the most important question: "Why do you want to sell this car?"

He answered, "I want to go to a graduate school. So I need some money."

His response seemed truthful and we understood how he struggled through pursuing an advanced college degree while his family was in Iran. After experiencing how he drove us on the highway and through town, we came back to the parking lot where we started our major purchase as students. We thanked him for explaining about the car and his situation. We told him that we would let him know whether or not we would buy it tomorrow. He thanked us for considering his car, smiled and said, "I look forward to hearing from you."

We walked back to our temporary housing without saying a thing. We both knew inside that we would buy this car because it was in good shape and the seller was happy to take $500 for it. We agreed that this transaction would help us and help him. We felt good in creating a "win-win" situation.

Now my roommate practiced driving all he wanted. After cleaning the dormitories all day long, we enjoyed dinner, and then waited until sunset to start the engine quietly, because a licensed person was supposed to be in the passenger seat to do driving practice. We were careful not to be seen by the campus police officers. Since this car had a manual shift, it took Winson a few days to get used to it. He practiced driving every night until our dormitory for the new academic year was opened. This included driving just to practice gear changes, acceleration, braking, parallel parking, starting on a hill, turning, safety checks, and so forth. We were like middle school kids sneaking in and out of the dorm, going to a dark parking lot to start the engine. We cracked up over not turning on the headlights, making squeaky noises for gear changes, or just driving too slowly. It was so fun and memorable.

After we finished the dorm cleaning job and had some cash in our pockets, we moved to the newest dormitory on campus for the academic year of 1987-88. After we settled into our room, Winson was ready to take the driving test. He wanted to complete it before the fall semester became busy. I knew that he would pass it. As soon as he got back from his test and opened our door, he asked me, "Would you like to go driving with me?" His face had a big smile. He had attained another achievement toward his ultimate independence and freedom in the United States. I was so happy that I was able to help him to at least get one step closer to his dream.

Serious Reason for the US College Degree

I respected Winson and Rosanna's attitudes toward establishing their solid academic foundation and building a career to create independent lives. I later realized that their study abroad in the United States had a serious and profound purpose for their life's plan. They knew that Hong Kong, which had been under the rule of British Empire since 1841, would be returned to China in 1997. This meant that Hong Kong might no longer be a free and democratic country. Consequently, their motivation to attain an education in the United States was absolutely necessary for them in order to obtain permanent resident status and become what is commonly known as "Green Card" holders. Then they would be able to become United States citizens. I felt that my purpose to prove my abilities with all my heart was a luxury compared with their circumstances. Their concerns were even more serious, since they had to prepare for leaving their motherland and settling in the United States.

In fall 1987, I retook the Dr. Markle's Anatomy and Physiology 201 with lab. This time I was ready for the Latin and Greek terminology—and anything else. As a result, I earned an A in both the lecture and lab. Dr. Markle told me, "I am very proud of you that you prepared yourself for a year to take this course again. Excellent, Shiro." My GPA in this particular semester was 4.0. I was awarded the highest honor as one of the top 3 percent of freshman students in the fall of 1987 and I received tuition, bookstore, and housing scholarships.

Fall 1988—University of South Florida

Finally, I stepped onto the soil in Florida—blue sky, palm trees, warm climate, and turquoise green Gulf of Mexico. I was so happy to be there with hopes of doing excellent school work at the University of South Florida (USF) in order to be eventually admitted into the Florida International University (FIU) physical therapy school in Miami.

At USF, I intended to take two semesters of chemistry and my third semester of the English course. Although chemistry was my least favorite subject, I was willing to be tested on how I would overcome the challenge. Since students who wanted to major in sciences, engineering, and health sciences were required to take chemistry, the class was held in a large auditorium packed with at least 200 freshman or sophomore students. I might have been one of the oldest students at 28 years old.

Dr. William Glosser spoke like a professional speaker with an incredible vocabulary, which even my American classmates had seldom heard. I still remember how he passionately spoke about how ancient scientists found "a speed of light." He was like an actor having a one-man show, as if the floor of the auditorium was the stage and we were the audience watching. We were fascinated by his unique presentation. He usually brought *The Wall*

Street Journal to talk about things other than chemistry. My understanding was that he was teaching us that "life needs balance." Chemistry was usually considered a laborious and boring subject. However, he made it so interesting that I committed to do all the assigned homework and more.

I was determined to apply myself better than before and better than anyone else. My strategy was to visit Dr. Glosser's office hours as often as I could with questions about lectures and assignments. Besides that, I neatly handwrote all the assignments, including diagrams, on used letter-size papers, leaving the other sides perfectly clean and usable. In other words, I made my own magnified study notes so that I could study anywhere and anytime without having to use my heavy magnification device. In the 1988-89 academic year, I was still able to study well by using pencils and a set of handheld magnifying lenses called a loupe; I only relied on the reading monitor for speed and energy efficiency when taking examinations.

Fortunately, not many people took advantage of Dr. Glosser's office hours. So I usually had his full attention for not only solving chemistry assignments but also having casual conversations about my academic goals, our families, and his favorite Japanese animations. As I asked questions about solving problems, he noticed my neatly handwritten problems with accurate diagrams.

He asked, "Is this how you study?"

"Yes, this is how I learn, by copying the problems in an enlarged way so that I can read without a magnification device," I responded.

"Are you recycling the papers when you prepare the study notes?"

"Yes, because the other side is perfectly fine."

I continued this method of studying chemistry for two semesters. As a result, we got to know each other well.

Despite my efforts and the professor's heartfelt help, I struggled, with grades hovering between a low B and a high C in both the first and second semesters. However, I eventually earned a B in both the fall and spring semesters. In addition, I earned an A in labs. In the lectures, mathematically I scored only 78 or 79 percent, which was a C. Dr. Glosser told me later, "Who doesn't want to give you an extra one or two points for your remarkable efforts?" I was so glad, because a C would have kept me from being accepted into any physical therapy school.

Fall 1989—Florida International University

I arrived at the Miami International Airport in early August. The atmosphere was different from any other city I had been in because there was a huge population of Caribbean Islanders, and Latin and South American people. I still had to take two semesters of physics with a lab, and one semester of statistics and sociology. In addition, FIU PT school required the General Science Admission Test (GSAT), which included mathematics, biology, chemistry, and physics. Furthermore, three letters of recommendation were required to apply for admission. After I completed all the prerequisite courses, I would finally be qualified to apply for admission to most of the PT schools in the United States. This was the American system. I knew it and I some-how had confidence that I would be accepted into the FIU PT school. At that time, the school had added a semester of a foreign language requirement before submitting the completed application. Fortunately, I didn't have to take it because I was already bilingual. So I started to conclude my fifth and last year of preparation to apply for admission to the FIU physical therapy school.

I struggled with the first semester physics class, which was mechanics. The professor utilized the chalkboard in the classroom from corner to corner, which hardly helped my learning style. Despite having a note taker in the class, I was not able to follow his instructions well. Once again, I sensed that I needed to drop the course because I could not afford less than a B, especially in science. After dropping the course, I kept attending the class to prepare for retaking it the following semester. After all, I had earned an A in sociology. As long as I was taking pre-PT, I was considered a sophomore, even though I had finished my fifth year as a college student in the United States.

In the spring of 1990, I retook Physics I with lab. This professor was different from the previous semester. He seldom used the chalkboard and he faithfully followed the textbook, from the introduction through the chapters. I felt that I would do well in this class.

Eventually, I finished the semester with a B in lecture and an A in its lab.

By the fall semester, I had only three prerequisites left to apply for the FIU PT school. So I enrolled in all three classes, which were Physics II lecture and its lab, and Statistics. The Physics II class was about electricity, which I only had a slight memory of from 12th grade in high school. So I was a little scared of the course. Although I knew that it would be a hard semester taking three science classes simultaneously, I wanted to submit the FIU PT school admissions application by January 15, 1991. This was the deadline for the new PT class starting that summer of the same year.

As I sensed at the beginning of the semester, taking the three science courses at the same time was difficult, especially since I had to maintain as high a GPA as possible. Two weeks into the semester, I decided to drop the Physics II lab in order to focus on the other two lecture classes. A science lab was usually a one-credit course; however, this one required at least three hours in the lab twice a week. To me, a lab was a time-consuming operation, whether it was biology, chemistry, or physics. Consequently, I focused all my energy on these two lecture courses.

In spite of all my efforts, I finished the semester with a B in the Physics II lecture and a C in Statistics. However, I still maintained a 3.75 GPA because approximately 80 percent of my pre-requisite courses were As. All I needed to do was apply for admission to the FIU PT school. I was so proud of myself for coming this far with some type of scholarship yearly, except for 1984, the first year of my student life in the United States. With that feeling, I almost skipped across the campus to hand-deliver my application to the PT Department's front office.

The Advisor

Since I arrived at FIU, I had begun meeting with Professor Lenard Elbaum, who was an academic advisor for those intending to major in physical therapy. I visited his office about twice a semester. After I had completed all the prerequisites except for the Physics II lab, I asked him, "Do you think that I can go ahead and apply for PT school prior to finishing my last remaining lab with the intention of taking it in the spring 1991 semester?"

He replied, "Since I know you have such an excellent GPA, it is absolutely fine with us."

I had truly enjoyed knowing him because he was communicative, pleasant, and humorous.

Most impressively, I felt that he showed a genuine interest in what I had to say and in my background.

Three Letters of Recommendation

I immediately arranged my letters of recommendation. First, I contacted my anatomy and physiology professor, Dr. Markle, at Northern Arizona University to ask him to write a letter of recommendation. He responded by saying, "Absolutely. It's my pleasure to write it for your admission."

Then I reached out to my chemistry professor, Dr. Glosser, at the University of South Florida. He said, "It is my great honor to write it for your successful admission."

For the third letter, I asked the director of the Office of Students with Disabilities, Dr. King, at Florida International University. She replied, "Of course. Who wouldn't write a letter for you?" Then I hand-delivered my neatly prepared application for admission to the FIU PT school during the first week of January 1991.

On another warm, sunshine-filled, 78-degree Miami day in late April, I returned to my condominium from school about five o'clock in the afternoon. I went to my mailbox as usual to see if there was any interesting mail. I found a thick envelope with the FIU logo on it. I thought that it might be from the PT Department delivering great news.

I quickly went to my room and turned on the magnifying reading monitor. My heart rate started racing as I neatly cut the edge of the envelope with scissors. I placed the envelope under the magnifying reading monitor and saw that it was from the PT Department. "OK, good," I said. Then I took a deep breath before I unfolded and placed the letter. The very first word stated, "Congratulations." My housemate wasn't there; room doors and windows were shut. So I shouted at top of my lungs, "Yes, I did it! Yes, I did it! Yes, I did it!" I felt that at that moment I got rid of all doubts from others, including my siblings and school friends in Japan.

Immediately, I began planning to see my family and friends in Japan for the first time since I had left Tokyo almost seven years ago. Why didn't I visit Japan for seven years? I wanted to keep myself hungry for attaining my first goal. In other words, I made a promise to myself that visiting Japan would be a reward when I reached my first major goal of being accepted into a PT school somewhere in Florida. The commitment was clear and absolute in my mind. That promise had already been imprinted in my hippocampus as I was flying back from the Oklahoma exchange program on a Northwest Airline Boeing 747 on May 5, 1983.

During my seven-year absence from Tokyo, many changes had happened in my family. My sister had married. My father had passed away. My family had moved to Shibuya from Shinjuku due to a road-widening project by the Tokyo government. I made travel arrangements to personally inform my mother that I had cleared my first major hurdle.

Short Visit Home

When I arrived at the Narita International Airport in late May, it felt good to breathe in the Japanese air as I stepped outside the arrival area. Then I hopped on a limousine bus to get home. I couldn't wait to tell my mother how far I had come. The clear blue sky and cotton candy clouds, the traffic, the tall office buildings, the typical two-story houses, and the landscapes that I saw through the window of the bus were all fresh and dear to me.

When I arrived home, I sensed that my mother was not wholeheartedly happy to see me or hear of the adventurous experiences that I was having so far. I also felt that my brothers were not exactly the way they had been, as if there was a dark shadow hanging over all three members of the Iwae family. In contrast, my sister was innocently celebratory and in a welcoming mood, preparing a huge sushi and karaoke party for me.

As I spent time catching up with my mother about what had been happening in the family for the past seven years, my mother confessed to me that she owed more than a million dollars to the Department of Treasury due to underpaid taxes from when the Tokyo government purchased their land and building for the road-widening project. The reason she owed such a large sum of money was because a tax accountant had made a miscalculation of the taxes she owed. She thought that she would easily be able to pay the difference on the taxes because the land and building had sold for millions of dollars. All she needed to do was to say that her accountant had made the miscalculation and pay the difference. Thus, she went to the bank to check the balance. She almost passed out when she examined it. The remaining balance was almost zero. My elder brother had used it all to purchase hedge funds without any communication with her.

As a result, my mother and two brothers as a group borrowed what she owed to the government from a bank. They could barely afford to back the interest on this bank loan. My mother did not explain to me how all this happened in detail, probably because of profound shame and guilt. I wanted to help her in any way I could. This unbelievable family crisis fueled my determination even more to be academically successful and economically independent so that I could one day deliver her good news and help her smile.

In summary: While I enjoyed my student life outside of coursework, I recognized the serious nature of keeping my 3.75 or above GPA. Therefore, I strategically applied myself diligently, assembled alliances and went the extra mile with the people involved. As a result, I received an acceptance letter from my first-choice physical therapy school, Florida International University.

Design Your Organized Planning

Ask yourself, *What are my strengths and weaknesses?* Then you will understand how you can design your own unique strategies for your enriching journey.

This process is to crystalize your desire into action. Therefore, it is critical to gather the most detailed and accurate information possible to strategize how to overcome many challenges for attaining your major purpose.

For example, I began taking the courses that felt comfortable for my level of English proficiency. Then I assembled note takers, readers, tutoring services, and testing arrangements through the Office of Students with Disabilities; I also kept the director of International Student Services informed of how I was doing. Moreover, I didn't forget to "go the extra mile" by turning in assignments a few days before the due date. It was beneficial for me to be acquainted with professors, advisors, and related school office directors and secretaries.

Can you design your own strategies? Yes, you can. You will make a world of difference if you start getting other people involved.

The steps in "Exercises for Your Dream" will show how you can design your own unique strategies.

Chapter 4

PERSISTENCE—
Continuing the
Extraordinary Efforts to
Produce the Results

Achieving your worthwhile purpose requires that you overcome many temporary defeats as you move toward an even higher purpose in life.

Once I was back in Miami, I was proud to start my first year of FIU PT school. I looked forward to going to my first class, Introduction to Physical Therapy, to meet all my classmates and professors. Every year, only 30 to 35 students were chosen out of about 700 well-qualified candidates. When I thought of those who could not be in the class of 1991, I felt responsible for completing the program and becoming a respectable physical therapist.

Before my first semester, which was summer semester, the PT school chair, Dr. Willie Huskins, asked me to visit her office. When I arrived, she congratulated me for being a part of the program and encouraged me to be a pioneer to educate all the people who might have doubted that a person with a visual impairment could become a respectable physical therapist. She was so excited about having such an unusual and challenging student in the FIU PT program. Her enthusiasm was a little overwhelming. But I knew that American people were expressive in general.

She proposed two plans for me to complete the program. Plan A was to finish it in two years, which was the regular PT curriculum schedule. Plan B was to complete the program at a little slower pace and graduate in three years. I knew that the regular program required 14 to 18 credit hours per semester, which seemed to be suicidal at this advanced level. So I told her that I would go with Plan B without any hesitation.

I kept receiving out-of-state tuition scholarships, and they continued until I graduated from FIU. Moreover, I seldom paid for learning supplies or books. I knew that I had a tumultuous three years ahead of me and I could not see the slightest light at the end of this tunnel. This was because the contents of the program would be highly technical and specialized. For example, as soon as the fall semester started, I had to take orthopedics, kinesiology, neuro-anatomy, and so forth. In addition, if I received a D as a course grade, I would be asked to leave the program. Scary, but I welcomed the challenge. To become a physical therapist in the United States, I had to seriously prepare myself with all the trillions of cells in my body. When I look back on my life, I see that I was almost always interested in pursuing something that appeared impossible to reach. In other words, I wasn't interested in grabbing "low-hanging fruit." I believed in pursuing romance and dreams.

Professor Karen Fisher

I would probably remember her name for the rest of my life. Karen Fisher taught orthopedics, which was one of my early courses in the pro-gram. Once again, a note taker and reader were all set for this semester. I was excited about being with these chosen classmates from differ-ent nationalities, such as Sweden, Iran, Cuba, Mexico, Haiti, Jamaica, and Greece. I thought that we were a very good group because we had one common goal: to become physical therapists.

Although I had taken many courses in English by this time, the many technical terms rooted in Latin and Greek for orthopedics were so unfamiliar that I felt nervous about taking the first test. Also, I felt that the expectations of the students were extremely high. So I took the test without confidence that I would earn at least a B on it. The result was handed back in the next class meeting. As I looked the test, I was shocked with the score because I had never seen such a low score in my American college life—62. *What?* I couldn't breathe for a moment. Then I thought of what one of the greatest Japanese Hall of Fame baseball players, Katsuya Nomura, said: "When you lose, there is no wonder." In other words, the reason was crystal clear why I did not pass the test.

Professor Fisher (we called her Karen) called me at home later that day. She said she wanted to discuss the test with me in her office. The next morning, I went to the College of Health building. As I entered it, I noticed that it was very quiet. That made me nervous, knowing that she might say something disciplinary about my test score. I gently knocked on the already opened office door. She kindly said, "Come in."

She was about 30 years old, with average height and weight. But what was most impressive about her was that she was always fashionable, as if she was ready for a photo shoot for a women's magazine cover.

"Have a seat. I have a few questions about the test," she said. "I think that you had difficulty in comprehending a subtle meaning of the questions."

I replied, "Yes," not sure exactly what would happen next.

She said, "Let's go over the test."

I nervously responded, "Okay," and I carefully took out the test from my backpack and handed it to her.

She pointed out three places on the test. I remembered these particular questions about being able to distinguish different types of spina bifida. She read the question slowly and said, "Tell me what this question is asking."

I explained what the question was asking.

She said, "Aha. I seems like you didn't understand what the question meant." Then she interpreted it for me without jargon. She asked,

"So what answer will you choose?" She slowly read the answers of A, B, C, D, and E to me.

I answered correctly.

She said, "Exactly," with her beautiful and encouraging smile.

I felt that she was not just helping me to pass the course, because college professors did not usually call a particular student on the phone about a test. She probably knew how shocked I was with the test score. So she called me at home instead of approaching me after class or stopping me in the hallway. She had sensitivity for protecting my privacy and pride. She believed in my potential to become a respectable physical therapist. I truly appreciated her thoughtfulness and her faith in me.

We went over the remaining two questions in the same manner. As a result, my official score on the test increased from 62 to 72. Karen gave me a big smile. She said, "I am so glad that you passed."

I was so happy; I couldn't help giving a big sigh of relief. This experience made me realize how much I had to improve my study habits for not only orthopedics but also all other courses to come. I reminded myself that I was in one of the most difficult health science programs in the nation.

I finished the fall of 1991 with all As except for a B in orthopedics. I stumbled with that course, but I recovered nicely. I continued to do well in the following spring and summer semesters of 1992 and I spent more and more time in the library taking advantage of the cool and quiet environment. Moreover, the library had a private room housing a magnifying reading monitor. So I spent hours at a time, at least six days per week, there.

The program was so demanding that the fall of 1991 and spring of 1992 flew by. More than halfway into the program, I kept an overall GPA of 3.50. I was fastidious about my grades because I had to keep my scholarships. More importantly, I discovered that having my mind set to such a high standard brought out enthusiasm and tremendous self-discipline, backed with emotions, which were the driving force for me then and for the rest of my life. I used to hear that people who became well-known for their achievements had clear goals, vision, and persistence. Thomas Edison, Andrew Carnegie, and Soichiro Honda were just a few great examples. By having a clear and purposeful target and dreams, I started seeing the light at the end of the first major tunnel, which meant that I would receive a bachelor's degree.

The First Internship

In the summer of 1992, my first internship began. Again, the internship coordinator was professor Karen Fisher, who taught orthopedics and helped me become aware of how I had to elevate the quality of my study habits by three or four notches. She did not tell me this exactly, but her gentle manner of communicating and believing in me touched my heart. I thought this was one of the best ways of inspiring people. Why? When someone expresses concerns sincerely by believing in you, you are moved. As a result, I started working harder and smarter in order to not disappoint Karen, and eventually it helped my academic success.

We were required to take on a total of five clinical internships—one at a rehabilitation hospital, one at an acute care facility, and one at a skilled nursing facility setting. For the other two internships we were allowed to choose whatever we were interested in pursuing as a future career. I saw this as an opportunity to see other parts of the United States. Therefore, I signed up to intern at Lee Memorial Hospital in Fort Myers, Florida, for my acute care training for six weeks.

During the 1980s and '90s, physical therapists were in desperately short supply in the United States. Consequently, most medical facilities were eager to provide clinical internship opportunities to students to enrich the entire American medical society that ultimately contributed to the world's health and education. The immediate benefit was that these medical facilities would often recruit students to be physical therapists at their facilities when their interns graduated. At the same time, it was essential for both educational and medical institutions to maintain good relationships. Therefore, most internship providers offered housing, lunches, and a stipend. Some of the remote locations provided transportation expenses, such as airfare, rental cars, or buses. My hospital provided me with a nice apartment that was adjacent to the hospital parking lot. It was an ideal situation for me to just walk across the parking lot to the hospital main entrance. But I became a little lonely, and nervous about how well I would perform and eventually pass my first internship in the real world.

Sunshine and blue sky—more typical Florida weather. I wore a half-sleeve dress shirt with a tie, a pair of khaki pants, and oxford shoes on my first day of work. I put my left arm through the left shoulder loop of my navy blue backpack and carried a long double-buttoned lab coat on my right arm. I said to myself, "You just do your best!" and I left the apartment.

I knew the name of my clinical instructor, but I did not know where the rehabilitation department was located. So I asked the front receptionist, "Good morning, where is the rehab department located?"

She said, "You go all the way down this hallway and you will see it."

A person with reasonable vision could say, "Thank you," with no further challenge. He could easily find the rehab department and he could even make nice eye contact with whomever he saw at the rehab area before seeing his clinical instructor. However, I always became nervous because I could not identify those small signs along the hallways that precisely read, for example, "Rehabilitation Department." So I required one or two more steps of asking others for help as I walked down the hallway. When I finally reached the department, I introduced myself to the first person I met and she brought my clinical instructor, Monica, to me.

She said, "Hi, I'm Monica. Nice to see you. You can put your backpack here and I'll show you around the rehab area."

I thought, *These people are warmed up and ready to go this early?* I would learn this was because physical therapists truly enjoyed what they did for a living and were proud of their profession.

The rehab gym was typical—about half the size of a tennis court with a couple of colorful mat tables, a few therapy balls, a set of parallel bars, a treadmill, etc., as well as some free weights along the walls. Across the hallway, there was a hydrotherapy room. After that brief tour of the rehab department, we sat down to discuss what we were going to do today and what I wanted to accomplish during my six-week internship.

Later that first day I was given a tour of Lee Memorial Hospital. It was a large general hospital with 415 beds. Most of them were private rooms. The cardiovascular and sports medicine departments were well-known. However, other medical services such as orthopedics, pediatrics, gynecology, emergency medicine, internal medicine, and so forth, were also offered. In addition, the hospital functioned as a teaching institution. Therefore, I came across many students from various medically related schools, including medicine, athletic training, occupational therapy, and, of course, nursing. Moreover, there was a fitness gym, library, and cafeteria for the employees. I thought that it was an ideal environment for me to experience my first PT internship.

My internship was in acute care. So my routine with Monica was to go to the patients' rooms to conduct physical therapy on the sides of beds. This helped patients to at least maintain and hopefully improve their physical strength and endurance while they were recovering from surgery, trauma, or illness.

Here was the daily flow of the acute physical therapy: The PT orders came to the rehab office from the attending physicians. Then we went to the floor of the appropriate nurse's station to double-check the PT orders in the patients' medical charts. After that, we read about the patients' medical histories and current conditions, including any medications they were on and if they had any family and community support. Sometimes we spent 30 minutes or so preparing ourselves before we visited a patient's room. If it was appropriate, we spoke with the attending nurse, social worker, and other medical team members. After all this, we visited the patient for the initial physical therapy evaluation.

We always knocked on the door and greeted patients. Then we introduced ourselves to ask for their cooperation to conduct the evaluation. In acute care, the patients were often very weak due to their initial recovery from various medical conditions. As a result, some of them were heavily medicated. Furthermore, monitoring and IV devices were often connected to the patients' arms and chests. I immediately learned to be extremely careful about even just getting to the bedside. From the very first day, I was determined to be the best assistant for Monica by doing things like clearing up the work space around the bedside and carrying a walker for the bedside exercises. For at least a week, my role was to observe how she performed physical therapy with these patients who were often half-conscious and undermotivated because of the difficulties they had been through.

During the days with Monica, I was extremely focused on everything I had to do. I needed to grasp a patient's information as accurately as possible by listening to what Monica read aloud for me, because I could not read the medical charts myself without a grandiose, heavy magnifying reading monitor. I carried a set of small magnifying lenses in my lab coat. However, they were hardly useful because they could only focus on one or two words at a time when speed and accuracy were required for the information gathering. Furthermore, I had to be very watchful in everything in the patient's room because the smallest mistake could be fatal to a patient and I didn't have enough medical or communication skills to deal with emergency situations. I did not try to think of ways Monica could help me a relax a little, or consider more suitable ways for me to practice acute physical therapy. Despite all the challenges I had to overcome, I was still happy to be where I was—almost halfway through the FIU PT program.

After my 8:00 a.m. to 5:00 p.m. daily training at the hospital, I went back to my apartment and quickly changed into swimwear. Then I went swimming, using all the types of strokes that I learned when I took swimming classes in

Kansas and Arizona. After I had enough exercise and relaxation, I returned to my apartment for a shower and dinner. I honestly do not remember what I cooked or ate during those six weeks. I was young—physically and mentally—and so focused on doing my best to pass my first internship. Every night I reviewed what I did that day and prepared for the next day by learning about unfamiliar types of medications, diseases, and insurance plans. I realized there were so many other things I had to know as a physical therapist.

During the second week, Monica gradually assigned me to part of the patients' care. For example, I performed joint range of motion, and transferred patients from beds to bedside chairs, or to bed mobility training. My internship was evaluated not only on its technical aspects, but also soft skills, such as an ability to communicate with patients clearly and respectfully. The internship evaluation sheet had more than 100 items to be checked off by the time I graduated. I thought that I was doing well, this being my the first internship. Then, during the third week, Professor Fisher came to the hospital to see Monica and ask how I was doing.

After finishing the conference with Monica, she asked me, "How are you doing?" with her usual sweet voice.

I said, "I am doing fine."

She said, "Good." Then she left for the next student visit.

At the end of the third week, Monica and I sat down to discuss how I had performed and what more I would want to learn about acute physical therapy. During the conference, she checked off a number of items from the evaluation sheets. In addition, she gave me complimentary words for many aspects of patient care. For instance, she thought that I communicated with the patients clearly and politely, and she thought that how I taught and led the patients through their therapeutic exercises was clever and motivating. Therefore, I finished with a good feeling that I would go through this internship without any trouble— meaning that I would pass it.

By the fifth week, I was able to go through the routines to treat patients appropriately, all while under the direct supervision of Monica. She even allowed me to establish plans of care for a patient or two.

At the end of the fifth week, we sat down to check off more items from the internship skills checklist. Monica said, "Good. Keep it up."

I felt certain that I would pass my first internship because I had satisfied all the required skill items. I smiled as I walked to my apartment each day and I went to the pool to keep to my healthy routines.

The last week of the internship I was asked to present something to do with the practice of physical therapy in front of all the rehab staff members. Since I had truly enjoyed learning about how to diagnose the 12 cranial nerves when I studied pathophysiology, I demonstrated all 12 tests in the simplest way possible with plenty of humor. My presentation was well-received. One of the PTs came to me afterward and said, "Your presentation had the quality of someone in the final internship of the PT program, not the first one." He shook my hand and said, "Excellent, Shiro." His encouragement inspired me to finish the final week strong.

Monica and I continued going through the routines of acute care. I began letting some of our patients know that I would soon finish my six-week learning experience at Lee Memorial Hospital and I thanked them for the valuable opportunities they had given me to grow as a physical therapist. Most of them were 40 to 50 years older than I was, and they gave me kind words of encouragement based upon lessons they had learned in life. For example, one of the patients said, "You will be a wonderful therapist. Keep believing in yourself." Another said, "Be prepared. Then you can deal with almost anything." It was a great six weeks.

I spent my last 30 minutes with Monica reviewing the skills checklist and looking for more skills to be checked off. She checked off a few more items, then said, "Shiro, good job."

I thanked her for being my clinical instructor. As soon as I said that, my mind was already on the final fall semester at FIU.

Futile Six Weeks

Two days after I returned from Fort Myers, I received an unbelievable phone call from Professor Fisher. I thought, *Oh, no. Again?*

It was bad news. She told me, "Monica failed you."

I said, "Karen, I satisfied more than all the required elements from the skills chart."

I explained that Monica didn't even suggest anything that would indicate that I had to improve more specific skills or that otherwise I might fail. I told her that Monica and I had sat down to check my skills three times during the six weeks and all she said was, "Good, keep it up." In other words, I said, she was not honest and did not tell me there was a problem or discuss with me a way to figure out a creative solution to pass the internship while I was there.

Karen said that when she visited Lee Memorial, Monica didn't tell her that I needed to improve my skills or that I might fail either.

The situation was all too familiar to me. Irrationality had happened numerous times in my life due to my visual impairment. I was used to being bullied in elementary and middle school. Unfortunately, it had now occurred in an educated, professional, and adult world.

Karen said, "Will you be able to come to my office tomorrow afternoon?"

I replied, "Yes, I will."

The next day I knocked on her already opened office door. She kindly said, "Hi, Shiro," with her usual smile. "Did you bring the skills checklist?"

I responded, "Sure."

She looked at all the pages of the check sheets. "Yes, Monica checked more than you needed to pass," she said with a puzzled face.

She looked down and began whispering, as if she was trying to find the right word to describe the situation we were in. "Not injustice, not unfair, FUTILE. That's the word," Karen stated. "I know how you are; you did your best to enjoy the learning opportunities and pass the internship. But she failed you anyway."

After a moment, she said, "I have a plan for you," as if she was determined to prove Monica wrong. "I want you to go to Jackson Memorial Hospital for two weeks. Then, if you do well there, you will pass the internship."

I was so touched by Karen's considerate accommodation for giving me another chance to prove myself. She was rescuing me again.

She said, "Go to the rehab department and ask for Curl Fernandez at eight o'clock on Monday morning. He is a really nice guy."

I said, "Thank you, Karen." I sensed that tears were coming, so I quickly left her office.

The Second Chance to Prove

As I rode on a special transportation vehicle to Jackson Memorial Hospital (JMH) in downtown Miami, I realized that the fall semester would start immediately after I finished these coming two weeks. I had continued schooling for eight years straight with a high level of intensity ever since I came to the United States in August of 1984. Many people had asked me over the years, "Was it hard for you?" "How could you keep it going without burning out or giving up?"

My answer was almost always, "It is a huge challenge, but it is such a joyful journey because America has a capacity to say 'YES' to the way I pursue my dream."

Like a boy playing with his favorite train set tirelessly, I had truly enjoyed seeing myself in the process of overcoming obstacles and growing into the person I wanted to become. My efforts and my indomitable spirit were the source of my power for the rest of my life.

I arrived at the main entrance of the JMH. I knew where the rehab department was located because my amputation and spinal cord injury classes had been held there before. I approached a person at the reception desk and said, "Good morning, I am Shiro Iwae from FIU. I am here to see Mr. Curl Fernandez."

She said, "Okay, let me call upstairs." Then she talked to someone for less than 10 seconds. She said to me, "Curl will be right down for you."

I said, "Thank you very much."

I waited a few minutes, feeling a little nervous because this coming two weeks might determine my future as a physical therapist. Curl approached and immediately recognized me. He said, "Hi, Shiro. Am I pronouncing your name right?"

I replied, "Yes."

He was so friendly, as if he was looking forward to working with me to fairly judge my progress as a physical therapy student. He was about six feet, two inches tall, with a medium build. More importantly, he possessed a presence, power, and warmth. Spending the first 30 minutes with him, I thought that I would be fairly evaluated whether or not I passed the first internship.

JMH was the third-largest teaching medical institution in the United States with 1,500 beds. The hospital provided a wide range of medical services, such as neonatology, pediatrics, orthopedics, cardiology, geriatrics, endocrinology, neurology, oncology, and psychiatry, as well as reproductive, internal, sports, and emergency medicine, and various research projects. Therefore, this hospital was a great place to learn all types of medical conditions; particularly, its spinal cord injury research was well-known worldwide.

My first day began by following Curl's caseload. The procedures were the same as Lee Memorial Hospital. We received the PT order and went to the nurse's station to double-check the order and learn about a patient by looking through the medical chart. Then we provided the appropriate evaluation and therapy.

Once again, my limited visual acuity did not allow me to scan through the medical chart as efficiently and effectively as others would. However, Curl found the patient's chart, checked it through, did the initial evaluation in the patient's room, and wrote up the evaluation in the chart in organized and legible writing within 30 minutes, all while other health care professionals were going in and out of the nurse's station like a busy commuter train station in Tokyo. This hospital was funded by the county, so anyone with or without medical insurance could be properly treated. Miami, often called a "melting pot of the

United States," is home to least 100 different nationalities. So, Curl told me, "This place is called a zoo."

Curl did not think that my visual disability was a big concern or that it would keep me from becoming a respectable physical therapist. He believed that physical therapy was not so much about doing things physically; it was a science and an art of work done by intellect. He whispered to me, as if he were telling his best friend the highest secret, "You can overcome this." He smiled, letting me know that I would be alright.

Another *wow* moment for me. My heart and mind were pounding again, and I struggled to hold back my tears. I was so moved by his encouraging words, and I was determined 10 times over not to disappoint him or Karen. I was nervous, emotional, and physically exhausted. But I was happy because I felt that I would not only pass the internship but also learn a great deal by working with him.

Curl's caseloads were mostly acute orthopedic patients. He let me do all types of therapeutic work, such as range of motion, bed mobilities, sitting and standing, balance practice, safety awareness education, etc. More importantly, he had me think about why a certain process had to be done or emphasized first instead of another procedure. For instance, patients recovering from major orthopedic surgeries had to learn bed mobilities first to prevent them from developing pressure sores. Actually, this rule worked for just about every acute case, such as strokes, amputees, spinal cord injuries, and all types of palliative care. I was very busy keeping up with the pace of this giant county hospital; we usually did not see the same patient twice. Younger patients were referred to outpatient rehab clinics and older patients were referred to the subacute rehab or skilled nursing facilities.

The first week flew by; I did not even notice what I ate for lunch. Younger medical staff—including medical students, therapists, and various technicians—were encouraged to use stairs instead of elevators to move from one floor to another. So we started seeing familiar faces as we ran up and down the stairs. We sometimes came across an attractive fourth-year medical student who could have been Miss Venezuela modeling swimsuits on Miami beach instead of looking for a patient chart in the chaotic nurse's station. Curl would make comments like, "Shiro, I think her skirt is too short for any hospital." He was trying to get me to relax, so that whenever I became too focused on passing the internship, I wouldn't forget to enjoy the whole experience at "the zoo."

Enjoying! This was the word I had heard again and again ever since coming to the United States. In general, we Japanese people take work too seriously; consequently, we do not associate "enjoying" with "working." However, I learned that these two concepts could merge and create a brand-new way of "WORKING." I believed that many American people live and work with healthy breathing space, optimism, and generosity, which is supported by the huge size of the country, abundant natural resources, a strong economy, democracy, and a tolerant culture allowing freedom to imagine and create.

I prefer to work to enjoy life. I thought about it a bit longer during the two hours of commuting between my condo and JMH. Here was my decision: In order to become the person I wanted to become, I needed to nurture an abundant mentality of believing that the world would offer plenty of opportunities, resources, and possibilities besides my becoming a physical therapist. With only four days left, I would broaden my horizon to start truly enjoying my life.

On Thursday, I encountered a most memorable elderly couple. The husband had had lower back surgery. We went into his room to educate him and his wife about bed mobilities and about donning (putting on) and doffing (taking off) his back and leg braces before he would be discharged to their home the next day. We practiced with him. He required minimal bed mobility assistance. However, he needed maximal assistance in donning and doffing the braces so that he could stand up and walk to the bathroom independently, which was his first functional goal.

After we demonstrated the procedure for assisting him, we asked his wife to assist him from lying on the bed to standing with the braces on. She reluctantly tried to assist him in donning the braces. Curl and I sensed that she had little interest in her husband's well-being because there was not a word exchanged between them during the procedure and her behaviors seemed to be obligatory. As we finished the practice and gave her instructions and precautions for assisting him, we heard an incredible question from her. She asked, "How long do I need to help him? Because I want to play golf." She said this in front of her husband.

Curl calmly answered, "He wants to be independent as quickly as he can, so it's up to you to help him become independent even quicker."

She looked unsatisfied with his answer. We left the room for the next patient. As we were walking down the hallway, Curl whispered me that a wife like her was called a "Jewish Queen." I understood what he meant.

In the afternoon, we came back to our rehab office a little early to go over my skills checklist. He did not have to check any skill on the list because Monica had checked more than the required number of skills earlier. However, he checked a number of interpersonal skills, such as listening to the patient, working with the patient with empathy, working with other health care professionals with a cooperative spirit, and so forth. Curl said, "I would rather be treated by someone with superior soft skills like you have."

"Thank you, Curl," I said. "This is the best compliment that I have ever received in my entire adult life."

He said, "Well, we'll go to lunch tomorrow. It will be your last day here."

I replied, "Yes."

The last day arrived for me to hear the result of my first internship at JMH. Curl and I went through the routine of the acute patients' therapy and evaluations. About 11:30 a.m., Curl said, "Shiro, let's go to the Bayside for lunch." The Bayside was a part of the popular Miami ocean-front, with restaurants and shops. From there, you could see the deep blue Atlantic Ocean and the many colorfully painted sailboats that were docked there. Curl took me to the most popular Caribbean restaurant there, which overlooked the bay on the boardwalk outside. I realized that about 10 white terrace tables and 20 chairs were set up. Suddenly, most of the PTs and rehab staff showed up to give a surprise lunch for me!

The internship had been only two weeks, and I had not come across most of these people because JMH was a large hospital and I did not work with either the outpatient or inpatient rehab clinics. I only knew one other orthopedic acute PT besides Curl. I realized that he had arranged the whole event for me as a good send-off. Everyone was cheerful end enjoying the sun, scenery, and food. I felt a sense of fulfillment about this summer of 1992.

Some of the PTs asked Curl about his three years in the Peace Corp in Africa. He had never told me that he had such a unique career prior to working for JMH. Now I understood his profound capacity to accept, tolerate, and appreciate people, and his attitude toward injustice, poverty, and prejudice in society. It all made sense why he was the way he was.

He said, "In Africa, you don't expect even a cane to be available off the shelf. So I used to go to the nearby bushes to find the most appropriate branch of a tree to make a cane for a patient. Of course, many people don't have money to pay for such a service."

He continued, "I was supported by the United States government, so most services were free of charge. But patients were so appreciative that they brought a smoked snake, a sugarcane, sunflower seeds, or whatever they could to compensate for their service."

One of the therapists asked him, "For how many countries did you work?"

He replied, "Three countries—South Africa, West Africa, and Tunisia."

Most people in the lunch event were fascinated by his African stories. After we ate and then ordered our desserts, Curl stood up and addressed all the people there about how he appreciated that we had come together for such a nice lunch and told them about my work for two weeks at JMH. Then everyone applauded. While they quickly ate the desserts before running back to the hospital, some of the PTs came up to me and said, "Good luck to you."

I said, "Thank you."

Curl took care of paying the bill and I thanked him for planning such a thoughtful event for me.

He replied, "You're very welcome, Shiro."

As Curl and I walked back to our small acute PT office, I expressed my sincere appreciation to him for allowing me to feel so comfortable and welcome. I packed my note pad and lab coat into my backpack and I thanked him from the bottom of my heart. As I shook his hand, my eyes filled with tears.

Curl whispered, "Shiro, don't cry."

I couldn't say anything, so I thanked him again. I hooked the backpack over my left shoulder and I left "the zoo."

On the way home, being tossed around on the special transportation bus, I summarized my first unusual internship experiences. Although I had spent six weeks at Lee Memorial Hospital, I felt that my two weeks of experience at Jackson Memorial Hospital was more moving and enriching because Curl treated me as a respectable human being just like anyone else. Furthermore, he considered me an individual who had unlimited potential to become a respectable therapist—with a little bit of ingenuity and smart planning. However, Monica at LMH saw me as a person with a limitation who was incapable of becoming a physical therapist. My sixth sense told me during those six weeks that she didn't believe in my abilities. In addition, she did not attempt to make my internship a positive and fulfilling learning experience. The truth would never be certain as to why she failed me.

I decided to become a man who gave people the benefit of the doubt, granting them a chance to move forward. At the same time, if I hadn't been failed at Lee Memorial Hospital, I would not have met Curl, who taught me what physical therapy was; he also taught me to be tolerant, thoughtful, and generous to people. All in all, I indeed appreciated the two opposing views of these clinical instructors who might have a great impact on my future.

The Last Academic Year 1992–93

When I showed up for the first day of my Pediatric Neurorehabilitation class, my note taker walked toward me and said, "Hi Shiro, how did your internship go?"

I responded, "I don't know whether I passed or not."

She said, "Don't worry. Someone like you always gets helping hands."

Soon Professor Suzan Davis entered the classroom, walked up to me, and asked, "Are you Shiro?"

I replied, "Yes, I am."

She said, "You have a message from Karen." She handed me a piece of paper with a message that said, "Please come to my office after class." I knew this was going to be the result of the internship.

As usual, her office door was open. I knocked on the door. She said, "Come in."

I said, "Hi Karen."

She responded, "How are you today?"

I replied, "I am fine."

At this point, I was still nervous about what she was going to say to me. She asked me to sit down and told me with a winning smile, "Congratulations. You passed the internship."

I said, "Thank you, Karen. I really enjoyed working with Curl."

"He told me that he also enjoyed having you. He told me that you were very conscientious of patients' needs and feelings; moreover, they liked you instantly. He said you would be a great physical therapist in the future."

I was so happy that I passed the first internship, which was two weeks longer than anyone else in my class. At the same time, I was so grateful that Karen and Curl gave me the second chance to prove that I could keep up with the FIU PT curricula. I expressed my sincere appreciation to Karen and I asked her to let Curl know that he inspired me and gave me definable hope to become not only a respectable physical therapist but also a man who would inspire others in the future.

In summary: I realized that I had to apply myself more effectively and efficiently than ever before because I scored a D on my first orthopedics test and failed in my first major internship. But I recovered nicely with persistent efforts and people who believed in my potential to complete the physical therapy program.

Develop Your Persistence

Ask yourself, *Is my definite purpose big enough? Is it worth pursuing it for my bright future? Am I enjoying the challenge?* If the answer to all of these questions is "Yes," you are likely to persist and achieve the life you desire.

Continuous effort is necessary to induce results and keep your focus on attaining all worthwhile achievements. Persistent action will inspire self-reliance, self-discipline, and creative imagination, and attract people who are willing to help you along your journey toward your definite major purpose. For instance, I had many difficult situations. But I always believed in myself and repeatedly said in my mind, *I can overcome this.* Then I overcame.

Can you persist no matter what? Yes, you can. Trust the power of your intelligence and wisdom to believe that you will get through and be a winner if you persist. Remember: "Don't take NO from someone who has no power to say YES to you."

Please refer to the "Exercises for Your Dream" section to develop your persistence. You will discover that persistence is the key ingredient to reaching your dream.

Chapter 5

COOPERATIVE EFFORTS—
Creating a Spirit of
Harmony with Others

"If there is any one secret of success, it lies in the ability to get the other person's point of view and see things from that person's angle as well as from your own."

—*Henry Ford*

My senior academic year started. I had only two more semesters on campus and three more internships to go. I finally started seeing a small light at the end of the tunnel. Although I knew that I had to put a great deal of tedious effort into completing the program, I had plenty of enthusiasm left in me. This semester was designed toward practical applications, as we were taking advanced science courses, such as pediatric rehabilitation, pharmacology, radiology, pathophysiology, and human growth and development. One of the characteristics of this semester was to choose a field about which we were interested in learning more. So we all went to our own chosen area of physical therapy practice every Friday throughout the fall semester.

Importance of the People Skill

I elected to learn about a private practice because I instinctively knew that dealing with medical charts in hospitals and other medical facilities was unproductive and difficult for me. On the other hand, I could design the record-keeping method however I preferred in my own practice. In addition, I enjoyed developing good, long-term relationships with all types of patients. So I began commuting to a medical building housing many types of private practices in downtown Miami.

In this private practice, I learned not so much about clinical skills, but about difficult aspects of running a business. Most private practices were reimbursed for the services they provided by the government insurance system and/or private insurance companies. In many situations, the reimbursement occurred two to three months later. For example, if a physical therapy service was provided on September 1, the payment for the medically necessary and appropriate service would transfer to the business bank account in November. This payment system drove the owner of the practice crazy. Even worse, sometimes the insurers denied the request to reimburse the service. Then disputes would begin between the practice and insurer.

I commuted to this private practice for a total of 15 Fridays in this semester. Almost every time I went there, the owner was hysterical on the phone with an insurance company representative about the denial to pay for a service. She screamed and cussed the representative. She usually finished complaining about the denial by banging down the receiver of the phone to hang it up. I understood her frustration because she needed to make a living. However, I knew that this was not the way to resolve the issue successfully. In fact, she had to spend too much time for telephone calls and resubmission or correction of the documentations to be reimbursed; sometimes she did not get paid for the service that she had already provided. Consequently, I ended up treating most of the patients on Fridays without her direct supervision, which was unethical and possibly illegal.

I thought that her practice would not be successful in either improving the patients' conditions or running the business. She needed to come from a philosophy of "touching the heart" whenever she was dealing with people. A famous Bible saying states that we should treat people as we wish to be treated. It is so difficult to be calm and considerate when you are under financial pressure. However, screaming and cussing at people is not the way to bring about a beneficial resolution. Most of the time, people are just doing their jobs. Even worse, we often express our frustrations and waste energy and time on someone who does not even have the power to say "Yes" and make our situation better.

In the book *Bend, Not Break*, the author, Ping Fu, was exiled by the Chinese government after its Cultural Revolution in 1960. She chose to attend the University of New Mexico and she majored in computer science. After she earned a master's degree, she started working for Bell Laboratories. While she was working there as a computer engineer, she received a PhD in computer programming. Eventually, she developed the first 3-D computer software in the world. Her initial motivation to create the software was to help the dentistry industry make dentures more accurately and quickly. Her software was so well-designed that a major toy company, Mattel, signed up to utilize it. Furthermore, because NASA recognized its superior quality, they employed her software for the Space Shuttle designs and maintenance program.

Now billions of dollars were at stake; Ping created jealous competitors, especially when companies that produced dentures and dental fittings attempted to take a piece of the pie. She began receiving letters threatening lawsuits. She consulted her friend, a corporate attorney, about it. She was so nervous about the lawsuits that she felt her life was in danger. The attorney said, "Ping, don't worry. According to these two letters, they want to discuss their share and their right to be in the business. Their survival is threatened by your invention."

She prepared herself 120 percent by rehearsing every possible question that they might ask her and any argument that they might provoke. She also rehearsed proposing a possible solution with her attorney to sit down and discuss an amicable agreement with those CEOs. She was still nervous the day of the meeting. Then Ping's attorney said, "Listen, two 6-foot-tall gentlemen with a certain social status will not mentally, and definitely not physically, intimidate a 4-foot-11 lady. Besides, you are in a much better position than they are, so all you need to do is listen to what they want. Then you sincerely show empathy for where they are coming from."

When she heard the attorney's advice, she was able to relax and calm herself down.

The meeting began without any sign of difficulties; the two CEOs were perfect gentlemen, as the attorney had mentioned to her. She asked them to speak about what they wanted under the circumstances, knowing that the 3-D technology would cause a big shift in the dental industry. Surprisingly, they wanted more time to figure out their corporate survival. All they wanted was to delay introducing, and possibly limiting availability of, the 3-D technology in the dental industry for a while. As the attorney had advised her, she listened to them and the strategy worked. They just had to agree on how long she needed to delay the marketing of it.

The owner of the private practice where I worked would have been able to drastically decrease the frequency of the insurance reimbursement denials if she took the same approach as Ping to prepare well, be calm, and listen to what the companies wanted. In fact, the owner could run the business with no insurance denial. However, she did not seem to take a disciplinary approach to run a successful business.

I do not remember what I learned there in terms of the hard skills of physical therapy, but I was beginning to believe that soft skills were more important for doing almost anything well. They were the things we could not see or touch physically, but were the abilities to be thoughtful, understanding, appreciative, and respectful to others. Patience, discipline, integrity, and so forth are essential to do well no matter where we belong in society. My weekly internship at this private practice was fruitful for helping me recognize one of the most critical elements for doing well in life.

In summary: I chose a private practice for my weekly internship. I learned few technical skills. However, the way the owner of the practice kept receiving insurance reimbursement denials taught me the importance of using soft skills for attaining fulfillment and success in life.

Enhance Your Cooperative Efforts

Having the skill of cooperation will make your life go smoothly, as if the wind hits the sail at the perfect angle so that the sailboat has a smooth and comfortable ride in the middle of the beautiful ocean.

Probably this is the most difficult skill for you to possess and use effectively to attain your major purpose. This is because you need to create harmony with others who have different values, belief systems, and cultures.

Andrew Carnegie, who established the United States Steel Corporation in 1901, became the richest man in the world. He later became known for his philanthropic work. While running the steel business, his most important role was to create "perfect harmony" amongst his chief officers from various departments, such as engineering, research, finance, sales, marketing, and human resources. He believed that the success of the business depended upon people working with a spirit of perfect harmony.

Your success depends on how cooperative people are with you and how you are cooperating with them. Can you set your mind to strive to create perfect harmony when you work with people? Yes, you can.

There is no end to honing this skill. Please refer to the "Exercises for Your Dream."

Chapter 6

POSITIVE ATTITUDE— Cultivating Favorable Personalities

A positive attitude touches people's hearts. It gives a pleasant and trustworthy impression; it also establishes equal and harmonious relationships, which brings you desirable circumstances for success.

We were encouraged to select three different types of rehabilitation settings to do three more internships before our official graduation in December of 1993.

The Skilled Nursing Facility

One of the skills that I needed to attain was to be familiar and comfortable with wound care. So at my first internship location, when my clinical instructor asked, "What would you like to definitely experience while you are here?" I replied, "I need to be able to evaluate, treat, and document wound care so that I can take care of such patients by instructing and guiding the assistants to be my eyes and hands."

My clinical instructor was Chris Taylor, who was also the director of the rehabilitation department. She responded by saying, "Yes, you will have that opportunity and I feel that you will become a well-respected therapist."

Whenever people said such complimentary comments to me, I sometimes positively wondered, *How do you know whether or not I will become a well-respected therapist?* For example, Doris in Oklahoma was the same way. She confidently said, "You can study and become a physical therapist in the United States" when I could hardly speak or understand English. Dr. Helen Henderson at the University of Kansas mentioned, "With your passion and definiteness of purpose, you can accomplish whatever goals you set." I was so appreciative to these people who gave me such encouraging words in a sincere way, and I believed their words and willingness to believe in me.

Most skilled nursing facilities in the United States were built in the 1970s. In those days, the concept of "rehabilitation" wasn't well-acknowledged or supported by the research data. As a result, there was little financial incentive to invest in rehabilitation departments when those facilities were constructed. Many rehab spaces throughout the country were not replete with enough space, equipment, or trained specialists. Nevertheless, the facility in which I interned had an approximately 40-by-90-foot, well-equipped rehabilitation gym; a hydrotherapy room; and a separate rehab office. One of the characteristics about this physical therapy department was that most of the staff members were physical therapist assistants (PTAs). Chris and I were the only physical therapists. One of the main differences between PTs and PTAs is that only PTs can legally perform a patient's initial evaluation. Consequently, Chris and I mostly evaluated new patients all day long, and then the PTAs rendered actual treatment.

Another unique part of this facility was that most PTAs were from South America or were second-generation Cubans. I was familiar with their general values, likes, and dislikes. During the first week of my internship, most assistants kept a certain distance from me due to a stereotypical view toward Japanese people. They felt a little intimidated because I was from the second-largest economic powerhouse in the world. They also believed that I was intelligent, highly disciplined, and diligent. One of the funniest moments was when I introduced myself to one of the assistants, Maria, from Ecuador.

"I'm Shiro. Nice meeting you," I said pleasantly, with a smile.

She said, "Very nice meeting you, too." Then she immediately asked, "What is your last name?"

I answered, "Oh, sorry. I'm Shiro Fernandez."

She began laughing so hard that people around us, including other therapists and patients, became curious about what was going on. She knew that I didn't have a drop of Latin heritage. The obviously incredible gap between how I looked and spoke, and the typical Spanish last name Fernandez, was hilarious. After that episode, all the assistants became very friendly and respectful toward me. Later, Maria told Chris about my last name being Fernandez when we were in the office finishing documentation. Chris showed me a cute smile that she had hardly exhibited before. I was then completely accepted by the entire rehabilitation team members.

Wound Care

Four weeks into the internship, Chris made sure that my skills as a soon-to-be-graduating physical therapist were at the appropriate level. When we were writing another evaluation at the office, she asked me, "Shiro, are you ready to practice wound care?"

I responded, "Yes, I am ready to learn it."

She began explaining about an 85-year-old woman with a just-below-the-knee amputation due to diabetes. Chris explained that she needed to improve her functional mobilities, such as rolling on the bed, sitting up to the edge of the bed, and transferring to a wheelchair. At the same time, her wound healing needed to be promoted by hydrotherapy, debridement, and compression bandaging. She said, "Let's go see the patient tomorrow, first thing in the afternoon."

I replied, "I will be prepared as much as I can."

She smiled and said, "Good."

The next day, Chris and I visited the patient, Mrs. Jones, in her room. She was neatly dressed, hair combed, and sitting in her wheelchair waiting for us. We introduced ourselves and explained why we were visiting her. She gave us a noble smile. She listened to our treatment plan intently and was willing to agree with our therapy program. Our goals were to keep her wound clean by hydrotherapy, debridement, and clean dressings of the stump. Once it started healing, she needed to come to the rehab gym for functional training, including bed mobilities, transfers, and stretching of the hips and knees for promoting as much independent living as possible with wheelchair use.

We took her to the hydrotherapy room to evaluate and clean her stump. While we were filling up the bathtub, Chris and I gently took the dressing off. It did not look raw and we observed no bleeding; we saw scab formations. In addition, she did not complain of pain when touched. We explained to her that she would put her stump into the bathtub water, which was a little cooler than body temperature, and the water would move around to really clean it. She nodded and smiled. I thought that she was truly accepting and trusting of us. I felt so appreciative that she was giving me a chance to practice wound care and gain confidence as I was becoming a fully independent physical therapist.

Chris was the type of clinical instructor who spoke little and observed me distantly. When she spoke to me or anyone else, she was gentle, caring, and trusting. Therefore, I was honestly able to let her know what I could and could not do in the wound care procedures. For example, I could not read the water temperature gage clearly enough to make sure the water in the bathtub was the right temperature. I also could not see well enough to tell what needed to be debrided from Mrs. Jones's stump. When documenting, how the stump looked and healed had to be described in her medical chart. Although I lived with numerous absolute physical limitations due to my visual impairment, I did not live with mental limitations. I told myself, *Hey, I can do a lot more things than what I cannot offer Mrs. Jones.* I knew how much water I needed to fill up the bathtub; I knew how to wrap her stump. More importantly, I felt I cared about her more than anyone else in the facility.

The next day, Chris said, "Shiro, if you can see the needle of the temperature gage, I will put a little piece of black Velcro pointing at the right temperature on the gage."

I enthusiastically responded, "Yes, that may work well," as if I had solved a complex math problem.

Then we went to the hydrotherapy room and tried it. It worked. My heart was jumping up and down, recognizing that I could overcome many difficulties with a little ingenuity. I understood that I could manage her wound care except for being able to clearly identify details about how the stump appeared. I asked Chris whether or not she could check how her stump looked whenever I worked with her. She said, "Absolutely." So the conditions that I could treat her independently were all set except for the accurate inspection of her stump healing process.

I went to see Mrs. Jones five days a week and she received hydrotherapy at least three days a week. For geriatric physical therapy, the treatment programs and schedules needed to be flexible because they are for elderly people who often have complications. Although Mrs. Jones' hydrotherapy only consisted of submerging her residual limb for five minutes, hydrotherapy could be very tiring due to the water pressure, temperature, and humidity in the hydrotherapy room.

In spite of being elderly, diabetic, and losing a leg, she was pleasant and respectful to such a young therapist. I was determined to give the best treatment to her for the remaining two weeks of my internship at this skilled nursing facility.

Mrs. Jones was very compliant with the therapy, including the functional exercises in the rehab gym after the hydrotherapy. About a week into the daily rehab routine, she whispered to me (as I always sat right beside her when she was putting her stump into the hydrotherapy bathtub), "It's hot." She immediately lifted her leg from the water. I checked the temperature gage; it had gone a little above the Velcro mark. I apologized to her that I did not double-check and check it again before allowing her to put her leg into the water. She smiled.

I told her that I would go get Chris or a nurse to check her stump. Fortunately, Chris was available. She inspected Mrs. Jones's stump and she observed how she looked in general. Chris asked her, "Do you feel any pain or any unusual sensation on your leg or anywhere else?"

She replied, "No, I feel fine."

Chris said, "Good, let's check the vital signs to make sure that everything is all right."

I took her pulse and breathing rates, then Chris took her blood pressure. Everything was within normal for her. Although we were a little in emergency mode, Mrs. Jones was pleasant and calm, as if she was giving us a message to calm down. "Okay, Shiro, you did everything correctly." Chris told me.

I apologized to Mrs. Jones again for my mistakes. I explained that I would clean her leg and wrap it. She smiled at me as if she was cheering me up. After this incident, she began asking me, "Is it mighty hot?" before putting her residual limb into the hydrotherapy lukewarm water. We looked at each other and smiled as an okay sign.

The last week of my internship came. Chris and I made time to sit together over a catered lunch in the family dining room to review my skills checklist. She immediately went to the wound care section and checked off most of them while commenting, "Good, good, good..." Furthermore, she checked off interpersonal and leadership skills. She asked me, "What types of internships do you have left?"

I answered, "I still have a private practice and a rehabilitation hospital."

She said, "I want to check off more, but I will leave them for those lucky clinical instructors." She continued by saying, "We indeed enjoyed having you. All the PTAs, nurses, and even social workers brought me nice comments about you."

I just quietly listened to her. I thanked her for her positive and thoughtful support in order for me to have the best learning experience possible. I also truly appreciated that she trusted me from the first day. I felt relaxed—free to be creative and to be myself to fulfill this internship for all the people who encouraged me to reach my dream.

The last day of the internship was always light in workload because all my patient caseloads had been taken over by the other therapists during the first part of the last week. I assisted all the therapists in the morning; then we had lunch together and I thanked everyone for making me feel at home in the rehab department. In the afternoon, I made time to see all my patients who had given me invaluable opportunities to become a fully qualified physical therapist. The last person I visited was Mrs. Jones. I knocked on her already opened door and came into her room. I cheerfully said, "Hi, Mrs. Jones," as if

I was greeting a best friend at a high school reunion.

She gave me a big smile and she began telling me about how well the leg was healing.

I said, "I am glad to hear that." Then I started explaining that today was my last day in this facility. Suddenly, oh no, my tear ducts began loosening up. I quickly told her how much I enjoyed getting to know her and spoke of my sincere appreciation to her for letting me learn a lot about wound care. Most importantly, I told her that I was so touched that she trusted me.

She calmly said, "Wherever you go, you will be great and appreciated. Thank you very much for taking care of me." She took my right hand in both her hands. I felt warmth and love.

The Private Practice

I quickly switched gears to my next internship because there was only a weekend to prepare for it. I almost always used special transportation to commute to the site of the internship and I needed to make a weekly round-trip reservation. I also had to prepare snacks besides lunch because the transportation was not always punctual about picking me up. In addition, it was a shared ride, so other passengers were picked up and dropped off along the way. I was always ready for that long ride home. The commuting time usually took twice as long as driving by car. Nevertheless, this community transportation for the disabled was great for me. It took me anywhere within the same county for a dollar each way. I did not think that the situation I was in was disadvantageous because during commutes I was able to immerse myself in listening to National Public Radio, planning for the future, and meditation.

In private practice, most clients suffer from chronic pain. Low back, neck, and shoulder pain are typical symptoms. The treatments are usually hot packs, electrical stimulation, massage, and exercises. The application of these modalities is called "symptomatic therapies." I found that these therapies did not show a continuous improvement toward either healing or recovery because they were unlikely to touch clients' hearts and minds to convince them to change their behaviors. In other words, rendering only symptomatic therapies did not lead clients to recovery. Assisting them to set their minds at the right place with positive actions was the foundation of true healing. However, it was difficult to provide such ideal services when the business structure was for-profit. I felt that Nancy, the owner of the private practice in which I interned, wanted her clients to be repeat customers, as if she was running a restaurant.

Ever since I chose health care for my career at the age of 20 in Japan, my attitude toward clients had been to help them as quickly and completely as I could so that they had no reason to come back and see me again. Therefore, I did not agree with Nancy's philosophy as a health care professional. Nevertheless, I didn't open my mouth to express how she needed to operate the practice because she could run her business however she wanted. Furthermore, I wasn't in the position to make such an unsolicited comment, which would never be for my benefit. So I treated all the assigned clients exactly as I was instructed to by Nancy.

Because I was originally trained as an acupuncturist, and as a therapist in shiatsu and anma (traditional Japanese manual therapies), most clients enjoyed the way I rendered therapies and answered their questions with the ubiquitous truth so they could heal as quickly and completely as possible. I became used to the daily routines of treating chronic symptoms.

I felt good about treating these clients because they were recovering. They were, for example, learning how to deal with lower back pain. Consequently, they were hopeful about resuming their lives and pursuing their dreams and happiness.

I was committed to helping someone progress in their life, even if it was only for 0.1 percent a day, because this meant that person could improve 100 percent in less than three years. In the Olympic Games, If a 100-meter sprinter ran 1 millimeter faster each day, he could improve by 0.1 second within three years. Thus, this Olympian would be almost guaranteed one of the three medals in the next Olympic games. I finally understood a bigger purpose of what I was doing for the past nine years. I was going to use physical therapy as a tool to make a difference in someone's life with all my skills and experiences, to help inspire people for building or rebuilding their dreams and happiness. I was neither perfect nor always inspirational. Nevertheless, I realized that I tried to offer something extra for my clients. The extra something meant that I was with the client 100 percent and that I was wishing them the very best outcome whenever I engaged in the treatment.

On Thursday afternoon in the last week of my internship, Nancy and I sat down together to review the skills checklist. She said, "All the technical and interpersonal skills that I thought you were superior at are already checked off. So I'll just write comments." After she wrote them, she looked at me and said, "Don't worry. You passed. You did a good job."

I said, "Thank you very much for giving me the opportunity to have these valuable experiences."

She replied, "You are welcome."

The last day came. I treated all my clients and told them of my sincere appreciation that they had allowed me to be their physical therapist to possibly help guide them to healing and recovery. There was no send-off lunch or any encouraging words from Nancy. It was a just another day at work.

The Rehabilitation Hospital

Black Hills Rehabilitation Hospital in Black Hills, South Dakota, provided one of the most comprehensive rehabilitation services in the region. From aquatic therapy for burn care to most services in between, the spectrum of rehabilitation could be experienced.

Outside of the facility was the famous national monument of the four well-known American president faces carved on the surface of Mount Rushmore. Those presidents were George Washington, Thomas Jefferson, Abraham Lincoln, and Theodore Roosevelt. Although I didn't know if I could visit the mountain, I was already seeing myself looking at those four faces before I even got to South Dakota. I had watched a film about the history and con-struction of the monument in my Listening and Speaking class when I took English courses at the University of Kansas. For all those reasons, I was excited about flying approximately 2,000 miles from Miami to Sioux Falls, South Dakota.

The hospital arranged a room at a nearby motel so that I could easily commute to the hospital Monday through Friday. However, the motel was not within walking distance to the hospital. Besides, walking or running across a six-lane avenue was awfully dangerous for me. So I made a reservation for a taxi to pick me up on Monday morning.

It was a nice surprise that the hospital looked like a brand-new structure with a beautifully grassed front yard. When I walked to the main entrance, the doors slid open and I walked into a tranquil space. I was assuming that there had to be a reception desk, but I did not see anyone around. Fortunately, someone who looked like a hospital employee walked toward me. She asked, "Is there anything that I can help you with?"

I replied, "Yes, I am here to see Lorain Larson at the rehab department."

She said, "Oh, okay. I will take you there."

So we took the elevator to the second floor and I encountered a typical question that often made me hesitate to answer. She asked, "Where are you from?"

Now there were two types of answers for this curiosity. I could say, "I'm from Miami, Florida," or "I am from Japan." Either answer was a correct response; however, neither answer would fully convince her. If I said that I was from Miami, Florida, she would wonder why I didn't look and speak like an American. If I responded that I was from Japan, she would be surprised that I had just arrived in Sioux Falls, South Dakota, from the other side of the earth.

So I explained, as her curiosity was gently calmed down, "I go to a physical therapy school at Florida International University in Miami, Florida. I am here to do my last internship before I graduate."

She said, "How wonderful. We are so glad to have you here in this hospital."

She appeared to be very satisfied with my explanation. We walked about 100 feet down a hallway and arrived at the rehab department, which looked like a well-designed school gymnasium. I said, "Thank you very much."

She gave me a smile and said, "Good luck on your internship."

Before I said anything to the closest person in the gym, I was immediately noticed by a young lady who asked me, "How may I help you?"

I said, "Yes, I am here to see Lorain Larson."

She showed me a big smile and said, "You must be Shiro from Miami."

"Yes, I am." I replied.

She said, "She should be back from a meeting soon. Please have a seat."

Within a few minutes, Lorain returned from her meeting. She immediately recognized me because she knew that I was scheduled to be here by nine o'clock in the morning. Besides, I looked like a typical intern, holding a lab coat and backpack, and sitting like a guest.

She said, "Are you Shiro?"

I replied, "Yes, I am."

She gave me a polite smile and said, "I am so pleased to meet you. Welcome to South Dakota."

Then my first day of my last internship began.

Lorain was different from my other two clinical instructors. Chris at the skilled nursing facility and Nancy at the private practice were both busy with the multiple responsibilities of running and managing for-profit businesses. Black Hills Rehabilitation Hospital, however, was a nonprofit organization. Each employee was able to focus on his or her own expertise and responsibilities. Lorain did not schedule any patients in the morning so that she could spend time helping me settle into the rehab department and make my six-week stay in South Dakota pleasant and comfortable.

First she asked me how I came to the hospital from the motel. I explained that I took a taxi. She said, "We must have a community transportation that the elderly and people with disabilities can ride within our county."

I said, "I am certain there must be one."

Then she continued to ask me questions about how I was going to manage grocery shopping, laundry, and leisure time for six weeks. At the end, she asked me, "Would you like to do sightseeing?"

I replied, "Yes, I would."

"Where would you like to go?"

I responded with no hesitation, "I would like to go to Mount Rushmore to see those four famous faces of the presidents of the United States."

She gladly said, "No problem, Shiro." Then she took me around to introduce me to other therapists in the rehab gym. Everyone was friendly and curious about Miami, Florida, because Florida is one of the top 50 states people long to visit to do leisurely activities in the warm weather. Florida is famous for its palm trees and Disney World, and is surrounded by the Gulf of Mexico, the Caribbean Sea, and the Atlantic Ocean.

After that, she took me on a tour of the hospital. This was the comprehensive rehabilitation hospital, but it was quiet and I came across few people.

When we returned from the hospital tour, it was almost lunch time. Lorain and I went to one of the two cafeterias where we joined other physical therapists and the director of the rehabilitation department. When we entered the cafeteria, the other physical therapists were already there to meet us. Actually, this rehabilitation hospital was connected to an underground hallway—which looked like a well-lit subway tunnel—to the Black Hills Regional Medical Center. The director and a few PTs worked there. Because South Dakota had long winters with low temperatures, wind, and snow, this medical complex was designed to withstand such climate. This was the reason why it was so quiet: the structure was well insulated.

In the afternoon, the director of rehab gave Lorain information about the community transportation system called "Rapid Rides." She told me that we would go to their office about four o'clock to make arrangements for my daily round trips to and from the hospital and to buy six weeks' worth of tickets.

Lorain and I got in her car and we went to the community transportation office. One thing I noticed about South Dakota was that it was not populated; therefore, we were the only people in the office. We were able to make the daily round-trip arrangements and purchase tickets without waiting.

After it was confirmed that my ride would pick me up tomorrow, we left the office and Lorain drove me to the motel. Many clinical instructors would say, "See you tomorrow" in the car and I would walk away. However, Lorain was different. She walked to the room with me and told me, "If you need anything to make your stay more comfortable, please let me know. I'll see you tomorrow."

Then I took a shower and ate while watching a news program on TV. After that, I organized my bedroom and thought about the coming six weeks. I slept like a baby.

The next day, the Rapid Rides bus came to pick me up on time so that I would be in the rehab gym by 8:30 a.m. The first week I was to get used to the rehab routines. I really liked their rehab gym because it was very spacious, horizontally and vertically. As I explained before, it was like a school gymnasium. The entrance to the gym was wide enough that two wide wheelchairs could pass one another. In addition, three powered large mat tables were arranged in such a way that a patient could access them from three different sides. Furthermore, all the small exercise tools and items, such as gym balls, weights, pillows, towels, and so forth, could be put away in the built-in closets. This was the most spacious and organized rehabil-itation gym I had ever seen.

Because Lorain was the only PT in the in-patient rehabilitation, she was happy to work with me as a soon-to-be PT. She and I first reviewed the skills checklist. She looked through all the pages and said, "I believe you can graduate from FIU tomorrow if you want." She gave me a friendly smile and said, "You work with me for this week. Then you will gradually work with the patients independently."

The Spinal Cord Injury

Lorain introduced me to a variety of rehabilitation cases, such as hemiplegia, joint replacements, and recovery from major surgeries. One of the most memorable patients was a young gentleman in his mid-20s with a C-6 spinal cord injury. This meant that most physical functions were paralyzed, except for partial upper extremity movements, and relatively good head control. Despite this major injury and disability for the rest of his life, he seemed to accept his reality and had moved on to what is called a "new normal." I was moved by not only his attitude but also his determination to get better for his family and, of course, his pride. I considered the cervical spinal cord injury was one of the most difficult case in the field of rehabilitation because such a patient could be totally dependent on the therapist for bed mobilities, transfers, and proper sitting position in the wheelchair. In addition, there were various physiological considerations, such as blood pressure, temperature, inspection of the skin condition, a catheter, and other medical complications.

The rehab assistant brought the young gentleman, Andrew, to the rehab gym. Lorain introduced him to me and told him that I would work with her as a team. He wasn't especially thrilled about having another therapist from somewhere he didn't know. I understood how he would not want to meet strangers almost daily when he looked so helpless and vulnerable, and that he wasn't thrilled to expose his injured, incapable, and not exactly clean-looking physical presence to another young man wearing a clean dress shirt, tie, and lab coat. This was why he wasn't pleasant when meeting me. Although I was not accepted by him at that moment, I was excited about this first rehabilitative challenge of the cervical spinal cord injury. This patient case was intimidating because he appeared to be at least six feet tall and 200 pounds. Furthermore, he required the maximum assistance of one to two people for transfers and bed mobilities. Thankfully, Lorain was stronger, more balanced, and more well-coordinated than I was when I moved around.

Lorain showed me how she transferred Andrew from the wheelchair to the mat table and demonstrated therapy routines. She also pointed out some of the precautions about the supportive devices that he was wearing to keep his lower extremities and trunk stable. At the same time, they especially helped with his veinous blood flow. After he settled in the middle of the mat table, I explained to him the therapy plan for today. He said, "Okay."

One of the most fundamental therapies is joint range of motion (ROM). So I started doing ROM exercises with his left leg. My impression was, *Heavy and resistive!* I felt that I was doing weight training with a 12-pound-dumbbell on both hands, because he was not only muscular but also spastic. My attitude for treating patients was to be with them 100 percent; my pledge to this profession was to move and use myself for them as the most important priority in the world. I knew that the therapy with him would be a hard road. But it was my pleasure to perform the ROM exercises of both the lower and upper extremities for him.

After finishing the exercise, we had a little conversation about our backgrounds. "Where are you from?" he asked me, as if the question had no consequence whether I was from the Earth or Mars.

I answered, "I'm from Japan."

Until I said that, he didn't show any interest in me whatsoever. Suddenly, I noticed that his face perked up, showing he was curious about what I said. He said, "I am a Native American belonging to the Sioux Indian tribe." He continued to explain that the Native Americans have Asian descents because some Asian people migrated to North America when Asia and the North American continent were connected through Russia.

I smiled and said, "I know about this because one of my note takers was a Navaho Indian in Arizona and she told me the same thing." After this conversation, he became friendly and respectful toward me.

The next day, he showed me how he was doing with the resistive exercises for the upper extremities and neck by using the apparatus fixed on the wall of the rehab gym. Because his trunk and both lower extremities were paralyzed, he had to train some of the unparalyzed upper extremity and neck muscles to be as strong as he could. This helped him compensate for some functional movements, such as bed mobilities, transfers, and sitting balance, and reduced the assistance he required. He asked me, "Can you think of any other exercises to increase my muscle strength?"

I asked, "Have you heard of the eccentric exercise?"

He answered, "No, I never heard of it."

I said, "May I explain and show it to you?"

He enthusiastically said, "Show it to me."

I explained that most of us believe that muscles are trained by shortening the muscle fibers exclusively. For example, the biceps curl resistive exercise is typical in training. However, muscles can be trained by lengthening the muscle fibers from the contracted position. So your biceps curl can be strengthened when you are slowly uncurling. In other words, your biceps can grow almost twice as fast if you are not just focusing on the curling action. Simply stated, you receive benefits of the resistive exercise throughout the "round trip" of curling and uncurling.

He said, "That's great!"

I said, "It's going to be twice as hard as only performing the one-way trip exercise."

He replied, "I can do it. Shiro, you are my coach."

I looked into his eyes and said, "Okay, we are the team rehab, Andrew."

After that day, we became the team rehab to achieve his hopes and dreams. He opened his heart and told me, "I want to go to college to earn a degree to better my chance of economic and social independence." Then he sought my opinion. "Do you think I can do it?"

I confidently replied, "Yes, you can."

I remembered seeing many spinal cord-injured students on the FIU campus and other college campuses. They realized that a college education could definitely help their future. It was ironic that 10 years ago I had sought out Doris's opinion in Oklahoma as to whether or not I could become a physical therapist in the United States. I clearly remembered, as if it happened yesterday, how she inspired me by saying, "Sure, you can." I unconditionally believed in her words, and now here I was a couple of months away from graduating from the FIU PT program.

Andrew and I continued to maximize his potential as much as we could before he returned to his home to resume his life. He improved his basic mobilities. As long as he was situated correctly, his bed mobilities were almost independent or required minimal assistance. Transfers required moderate to maximal one-person assistance with a sliding board. Sitting balance became independent to minimal assistance without holding the armrests or leaning against the backrest of the chair; in other words, he could hold himself at the edge of the mat table for a few minutes safely.

I thought that he had almost reached his long-term physical therapy goals. I complimented him on showing incredible determination to move forward toward his future. I also told him that I was impressed by his discipline to deal with not only physical and occupational therapies, but also medical complications and the uncertainty of the next 50 or 60 years of his future. Then I told him that he would be discharged from PT soon and I appreciated him giving me such wonderful opportunities to get to know him and learn about his C-6 incomplete spinal cord injury rehabilitation.

Four Faces on the Rock

My last internship had only one week left when Lorain asked me, "Would you like to go to Mount Rushmore this weekend?"

I enthusiastically answered, "Yes, I would."

She smiled and said, "All right. I will pick you up on Saturday morning about 11 o'clock."

I smiled and told her, "Thank you, Lorain. I really look forward to it."

It was mid-October. South Dakota was already in late fall, which was nice and cool in the mornings. Lorain showed up at my door with a fall jacket, jeans, and boots; she was ready for driving up to the mountain of 5,700 feet. Since I did not like to feel cold, I also properly dressed for it.

She had a blue GM mid-sized car, which was very spacious and comfortable inside. Driving up almost any mountain was a slow process of going about 10 to 20 miles per hour because you could only use first or second gear. This speed was just right to enjoy the beautiful autumn landscape. After 50 minutes of driving up to the observation deck to see the famous sculptures of Washington, Lincoln, Adams, and Roosevelt, we walked up to the closest viewing point, which was about 150 yards away and 45 degrees above us.

I suddenly became emotional because I had watched the documentary film about the construction of this monument when I was at the University of Kansas. At that time, I was only six months into this incredible journey, setting my purpose to become a physical therapist but not knowing exactly how or when such a day was coming. Nine years later, here I was, actually standing in front of these faces carved in the surface of this mountain, finishing my last semester of a physical therapy program.

We walked toward Lorain's car and started driving down the mountain. Going down the winding road was also a slow process, because she had to control the car by applying the brakes properly and handling the curves. Here I was again looking out the window, enjoying the scenery and knowing that I would not visit this mountain again. I did not remember how many times I had sat on the passenger seat of someone's car since I came to the United States. I almost always enjoyed the rides because there were no traffic jams like in Tokyo. The highways and major roads were wide and mostly straight, looking toward the horizon. Along the drive, I could see beautiful forestry and wide-open rolling hills, sunflower fields, and other agriculture lands for miles and miles. I could make such an innocent comment because I had never experienced the responsibilities of driving. I enjoyed sitting in the passenger seat as if I was a royal guest who was totally well taken care of.

Lorain said, "We are home." She pulled her car gently into the parking spot closest to my room at the motel. She turned off the engine and got out of the car to walk with me toward the door, making sure that I safely arrived in the room where I had been staying for the last five weeks. She smiled and said, "I'll see you on Monday."

The final week of my internship began. The last weeks were usually great, as I got to tell as many past and present patients as possible that I wholeheartedly appreciated their being my patients so that I could become a fully qualified physical therapist. Most of my patients were at least 40 or 50 years older than I was. Despite their medical conditions, they gave me words of wisdom or encouraging words while looking into my teary eyes. I had probably secreted a gallon of tears since I was accepted into the FIU physical therapy program.

On Thursday, Lorain and I sat down to go over the skills checklist. She said, "Most skills are already checked. Let me write something in the comments section."

Whenever anyone said that, my heart pounded. I knew that I was one of the students chosen to be in this highly competitive professional program and that I was in the enviable position where I could pick and choose an ideal environment to practice physical therapy as soon as I passed this internship. But I always had a sense of being the last qualifier in any group to which I belonged academically. In other words, I always had the feeling I wasn't good at academic performances growing up. I felt that this was my trauma, which I would carry all my life.

Lorain finished writing a few comments while these insecure thoughts were going around in my mind. She said, "Do you want me to read them for you?"

I knew that she wouldn't write highly critical comments, but my response of "Yes, please," wasn't confident.

She read, "Shiro is one of the most caring, conscientious, and intellectual people that I have ever met. His disabilities are not disabling him;

they are unique tools that enable him to excel at whatever he may decide to endeavor to do in the future. I highly recommend that he pass this internship and I congratulate his honorable achievements."

Here came my tears. I could hardly voice my "Thank you for everything" to her. She gently hugged me. I felt a little embarrassed; my life always seemed to be furnished with dramatic beginnings, middles, and finishes.

The last day came. All my patients were already assigned back to Lorain. So my last bit of work was to finish up paperwork and clean up the desk for the next person using it. At the same time, I made myself available to assist anyone at any time. Of course, there was a farewell lunch. When Lorain and I arrived at the cafeteria, a large table was set; probably 10 people could sit around it easily. Then here they came. Most of them were acute and outpatient physical therapists from the medical center. I had only met them once at the first welcome lunch. But they were very friendly while they had worked with me for the past six weeks. Everyone congratulated me for finishing the last internship and soon graduating from the FIU PT program. They shook my hand and gave me hugs. These people were very sincere because they knew how difficult it was to be accepted into the program and complete it. I very much like these respectfully friendly American people. This was one of the reasons why I had spent the best part of my 30 years of life in the United States.

I thanked everyone in the rehab department, including occupational and speech therapists, and all the assistants. Lorain saw me off and waved her hand until my community transportation disappeared from her sight. It was a short five-minute ride to my motel; nevertheless, my mind was already busy scheduling a number of interviews for prospective employers. As soon as I stepped off the bus, I walked to the motel office. I thanked the manager who had arranged the weekly coin laundry trips and grocery shopping for me. I told her, "I will fly back to Miami tomorrow."

She said, "We really enjoyed having you here. How are you going to get to the airport?"

I replied, "I will call a taxi tonight to make a reservation."

She kindly told me, "Don't worry, we will take you there."

I said, "Thank you very much."

This type of thoughtful offer had happened countless times since my American life started. I wondered whether or not I was transmitting something that caused people to want to give me help. This was how I continued to overcome many difficulties. Throughout my life, someone was always there to encourage and inspire me going forward as I pursued my dream.

In summary: During my last three major internships, I made an honest effort to understand patients and address their functional recovery. At the same time, I genuinely appreciated all the patients and clinical instructors who had helped me become a respectable health care professional. I had finally completed the entire physical therapy program for my official graduation.

Build Your Positive Attitude

As you begin the journey for your dream, you will come across rainy days. If you have the ability to think about the bright aspects of rain, which nurtures vegetation, fish, animals, and our earth, your life will be abundant and fulfilled.

A positive attitude is the single most important quality in the science of success. When you meet someone who demonstrates a positive attitude, you receive a good impression of them. This in itself gives you many advantages to achieve what you want in life. For example, if you are pursuing your major purpose with a positive attitude, people around you will often be attracted to you and help you reach your dream. Moreover, a positive attitude not only attracts favorable attention, but also repels things you do not want. This is the power of a positive attitude. Can you develop and practice it? If so, you will see and feel a world of difference. Pleasant smiles, a good posture, and a firm handshake will be great starting points for you. Can you start building it? Yes, you can.

"Exercises for Your Dream" will show you how positive attitudes can be built. The benefits are all yours.

Chapter 7

APPLIED FAITH— Sustaining Belief in Action for Attaining Your Definite Purpose

You are the master of your life. If you believe, you shall achieve. The dream becomes the reality.

On the airplane back to Miami, I felt a good sense of accomplishment and looked forward to the next challenges of building my career as a physical therapist. Of course, I listened to *Big Wave* by Tatsuro Yamashita all the way to the Sunshine State.

Special Advice

When I returned to Miami, the first thing I wanted to do was to see Karen and the chair,

Dr. Haskins, to inform them that I had success-fully completed all my internships. Karen was so happy that I had passed them without any problems. After I wholeheartedly thanked her, I visited the PT department chair's office. She was also very excited about my finishing the entire PT program. I thanked her for giving me this once-in-a-lifetime opportunity to have such valuable and memorable experiences these past three years.

She walked to the door purposefully and closed it. She slowly walked back to her desk and sat down in her chair. She gave me a big smile, like a proud mother looking at her son at college graduation. She said, "Congratulations! You did it."

I replied, "Thank you very much for giving me such precious and life-changing opportunities. I will become a respectable physical therapist who can make a difference in the lives of others."

She gave me another big smile and asked, "Have you started searching for your employ-ment opportunities?"

I answered, "I intend to start doing so today or tomorrow."

She said, "Good." I sensed that she was going to give me some advice before contacting prospective employers. She looked at my face squarely with a rather serious tone of voice and said, "Shiro, do not tell or write to them about your visual disabilities until you are in a face-to-face interview or when you tell them of your decision to work for them. If you tell them about your disability before they actually meet you, they will have a preconceived idea about you. However, when they meet you in person, they will fall in love with you. Then tell them what you need to function well as a physical therapist. Now, Shiro, go out and become the pioneer to educate all of us about how small changes and a little ingenuity will make someone like you as functional as others without disabilities."

I completely understood her honest advice and expectation of me. I thanked her again. We stood up and shook hands firmly.

I finally decided to begin my career in the eastern suburb of Seattle, Washington. It offered the shortest flight to Tokyo. In addition, I preferred to live in a smaller, inexpensive community so that I could get around the community easily and save money. At the same time, I would have great access to a major international airport servicing many destinations worldwide. Now I needed to find an employer and apartment within walking distance of each other. I knew that a geriatric rehabilitation setting was suitable for me because I truly enjoyed my grandmother and understood how elderly people thought and functioned as they aged. Furthermore, I couldn't help but respect them for their contributions to building a better society for younger generations. I felt a sense of duty for requital as a favor to them through my profession.

I was a decade away from being able to do a "Google search" or logging onto a specific website to look for employment opportunities. At that time most people relied on magazine and newspaper ads, or someone they knew in a profession, to find a prospective employer. In my case, I looked at the "PT Bulletin" published by the American Physical Therapy Association. There were so many hospitals, clinics, and companies desperately recruiting physical therapists by offering competitive salaries, big sign-on bonuses, relocation expenses, a full package of health and life insurance, and a retirement plan. However, I was not attracted to those incentives. I knew that things almost always came down to the quality of the people with whom I worked. I began contacting a company called Hill Haven, which provided skilled nursing care along the Northwestern Coast of Washington.

I decided to call their corporate office to find out what was available for a new graduate. The recruiter responded enthusiastically and explained that they were trying to fulfill one physical therapist position in Puyallup, Washington. I told her that I was interested in the location and would like to be interviewed. She said, "That is great! Would you be able to fax or mail your resume?"

Once again, electronic communication was a decade away from common use. So I mailed my resume to the Hill Haven Human Resources Office. It took about four days for me to receive a phone call from the recruiter. She said, "Thank you for sending us your resume. We will set up the interviews and your travel arrangements, including the airlines and hotel."

The Job Interview

In 1993, we were still able to wait for someone at a gate of an arriving airplane. When I came out of the jetway in Seattle, a young woman walked toward me and asked, "Are you Shiro?"

I answered, "Yes, I am."

She said, "Welcome to Washington. I'm Carol."

We shook hands with friendly smiles. Then she led me to her car and she drove me to the location in Puyallup, Washington, which was about a 30-minute drive east of the airport. It was beautiful to see tall and straight trees creating deep green forests along both sides of the highway. The western part of Washington received rain about 150 days a year. Consequently, many types of plants and trees grew well in this part of the country. When we got off the highway, Carol said, "We are arriving at the Rainier Vista Nursing Center."

It was just before the Thanksgiving holidays. As I stepped into the main lobby of the facility, a beautifully decorated eight-foot Christmas tree caught my eye. Thanksgiving through Christmas was one of the most emotional, joyous, and memorable times of the year for me because Hop and Doris in Oklahoma always invited me to stay in their home to celebrate these holidays.

I was led to a small conference room to wait for the director of rehabilitation for the interview. A few minutes later, the director knocked on the door and came into the room; I immediately stood up and introduced myself. She gave me a smile and said, "I am Margarete. It is nice meeting you." We shook hands and sat down at opposite sides of the table. She opened her file, which I assumed contained my resume, the interview questions with the evaluation, and comments spaces. She appeared well-prepared to recruit me.

She began asking why I chose to work in an elderly rehabilitation setting. I explained that I could understand how elderly people thought and felt because my grandmother was my best friend and gave me unconditional love and support as I grew up. I wouldn't be able to return a favor to her, but I could give all I had to enhance the quality of older people's lives as a physical therapist.

She nodded and wrote something down. Then she asked me why I preferred to work in this part of the country. I answered that I would have good access to Tokyo; more importantly, Puyallup, Washington, was the right size of city for me to live in. She again nodded, as if she was convinced by my explanations. She said, "Let me show you around the facility and introduce you to our staff members."

So I followed her around. I had learned that the quality of nursing facilities could be distinguished by human waste odor. Nursing facilities are known to have a distinctive smell, due to the fact that most residents are diaper-dependent. However, I did not smell that type of distinct odor here. The hallways were appropriately lit and clean; framed decorative paintings were along the walls. I thought the facility was well-managed by a conscientious leader.

She said, "Here is the rehab section of the facility." Rehabilitation services were a fairly new concept in nursing services at that time. Therefore, rehab departments were usually located at the end of a hallway or a basement, and seen as a nonpriority, complementary role of elderly medical services. However, this section of the building did not look as if it had been added later; it looked planned from the beginning of the architectural design because the nursing station, which overlooked the rehab gym across the hallway and the patients' rooms, extended all around these two main parts of the rehab department. Moreover, the rehab gym was well-lit and designed to take in as much natural light as possible by having wide windows that ran the complete length of the south side of the gym overlooking the courtyard.

Since the therapists were busy with their afternoon treatments, she took me to the rehab office to introduce me to the manager, Nena, who was the only evaluating PT. She was friendly and even told me that she drove a Subaru. While we were conversing in the office, one by one, the staff members came back after finishing their treatments with patients. So I was introduced to all the therapists and rehab assistants. I suddenly realized that I was the only man in the entire rehab department. After finishing all introductions and friendly conversation, Margarete explained that Carol would take me to dinner and drive me to the hotel.

The Advice Was Tested

As soon as I came back home in Miami, I began planning to move to Puyallup, Washington, to take the job opportunity at the Rainier Vista Care Center. The next day, I called Margarete and told her that I wanted to work in their facility. She sounded very happy that I chose her rehab team. Since I sensed her enthusiasm, I told her about my visual impairment requiring a magnifying reading monitor for paperwork and other assistance that would be necessary for accurate vision, such as wound care.

There was a pause on the other side of the phone, which made me think I would be getting a negative answer from her.

Margarete asked, "What else do you need?"

She sounded as if all the expenses and accommodations did not bother her a bit. In other words, she was expressing that my potential contributions to the rehab team for ultimate quality health care services were far more valuable than the initial cost and assistance coming with my employment. I thought that Dr. Haskins had given me the right advice. I felt excited about moving to Washington, and I learned a strategy that I could keep utilizing in many years to come.

Now my life was going toward the next stage of career-building and independence. The most important factor was to find an apartment located within a short and safe walking distance from my work. Why? I was not able to drive a car; in addition, I noticed that I had started limping with my right leg just little. So I contacted several real estate offices to list my specific needs. The nicest reply was from Claudia Maives, a real estate agent for Coldwell Banker. Normally, these agents would help people find homes, not apartments. This was because helping to find an apartment for me did not make a dime for them.

Nevertheless, Claudia was willing to meet my needs. When I arrived at the American Airlines gate at the Seattle-Tacoma International Airport, she was waiting for me, standing straight, with a friendly smile. Why did I notice her with my limited vision, since I was the last person to come out of the airplane? By the time I walked through the jetway, no one was around but her, and she asked, "Are you Shiro?"

I answered, "Yes, I am." This was the beginning of our long-lasting friendship for decades to come.

As we were walking to the airport parking, she asked if I had a nice flight and she explained the typical fall weather in Northwestern Washington; moreover, she told me about the people, cultures, industries, and sports in the area. When we started driving, I asked her, "What kind of car is this?

"Nissan Maxima," she proudly answered. "I like the Japanese cars."

I knew that Japanese cars were popular because of their reliability and fuel efficiency. While we were driving to Puyallup, she explained that we were going to look at a few apartments. She sounded well-prepared and confident. I hardly remember what we conversed about in the car after that, but I sensed that I could trust her because of her professional look, and her friendly and honest manner.

First she drove to the facility where I would work. Then she drove to the apartments that she had chosen for me. Why did she do that? She wanted to measure the approximate distance from my work to them. Along the way to each apartment, we carefully observed whether or not I could walk to work safely. I saw some housing less than one block away from the facility. Claudia said, "You don't want to live there." I understood what she meant; living in a certain neighborhood determined safety of living and, unfortunately, social class. Now I surely knew that she was 100 percent on my side.

We arrived at the first apartment. It was a beautiful-looking place to me, with light brown wood floors, off-white walls with green trim, and 18-foot ceilings that perfectly allowed for optimal natural light to keep the space warm and cheerful. In addition, this apartment was close to restaurants, shops, and grocery stores. But it was not located within walking distance to work. Although I could use the community transportation for the disabled, it was important to me that I be as independent as possible. So we drove to the next property.

The next one was as nice as the previous one; however, it was not located within walking distance from my work either. Consequently, we drove again to a third property. I realized that Claudia had started showing me the farthest properties from my work and then ones back closer to it. The last apartment was called "Kenbridge." I liked the name of the apartment. Moreover, there was a property management office on-site, and the manager was in the office 365 days a year for the residents. The manager was friendly and helpful, showing us the one-bedroom unit closest to the entrance of the property. The interior of it was nothing like the first one. It was an ordinary apartment, which meant about 50 percent more space than a modern college dormitory. Since the most critical factor in housing for me was to be able to walk to my work, it didn't take long to decide what to choose among those three properties.

By the time I signed the rental contract, it was already dark outside. We suddenly felt hungry. Claudia suggested we go to a local Japanese restaurant. Even though she had driven by the restaurant many times, she had not been there. So she was excited about trying Japanese food for dinner. Since we had been together all afternoon, she really understood how my visual impairment was. So she read the menu aloud and explained where the green tea, water, napkins, and chopsticks were on the table with a friendly and caring tone of voice. She seemed to be enjoying spending the day with me.

Three decades later, Claudia and I are still in touch by emails. She told me later how she felt when she received a referral to pick up a client from the airport. She was informed that I had a "handicap," but was given no details. That left her wondering what she was going to be doing. As it turned out, all her fears were relieved after meeting me and getting acquainted. This proved that Dr. Haskins was right about not informing people of my disabilities prior to actually meeting them in person, because most people have preconceived ideas about the words "handicap" or "disability." To this day, I practice her advice when it is appropriate.

Many people, especially my Japanese friends, likely wondered why I had chosen such an unimaginable and challenging life. It would be extremely hard for even a nondisabled person to overcome all the required and necessary steps to attain an education, college degrees, employment, and licenses in a different culture and language. However, I thrived in doing this because I felt totally free from the stereotyping, limitations, and impossibilities that Japanese society had imposed upon me. At the same time, I was definitely committed to proving them wrong. Most importantly, I was thrilled by and enjoying every single day of my life in the United States.

The Moving and Building Career

I wanted to move to Washington before it got really cold. The most important process of leaving Miami was to let people who had helped me along the way know how much I appreciated them. I thanked all the professors at the FIU PT Department, all my note takers and readers, the director and secretary of the Office of Disabled Students Services, and close friends. I truly believed that I could not have earned my bachelor's degree without these people who were willing to reach out and assist me with whatever I needed to succeed.

The airplane landed at the Seattle-Tacoma International Airport. My heart began pounding, anticipating starting my new life and seeing Claudia again. She was right there at the gate, in the same position where she had waited for me a few weeks ago. She looked happy to see me again. "Welcome back to Washington!" she said with a big smile.

I thanked her from the bottom of my heart. I was extremely touched that she was picking me up at the airport, driving me to Puyallup, and getting me settled in my apartment for no financial gain as a real estate agent.

Moreover, she asked me, "Do you have something to eat for tonight?"

I answered, "No, I don't."

So she took me to buy a few things until I could go on a major grocery shopping trip. And, of course, she was the one who took me on this major shopping trip the very next day. For the next six months while I lived there, she not only took me grocery shopping almost every week, but she also carried a bag or two of groceries to my apartment on the second floor. We occasionally had dinner at that Japanese restaurant.

Permanent Physical Therapist License

Most PT graduates would start working with their temporary licenses, assuming that they would pass the bord examination. After I had worked at the Rainier Vista Care Center for a couple of weeks, I took the Washington State Board Examination for Physical Therapy.

There were two people I had to inform about the unexpected result. The following morning after receiving the result of the licensure examination, I asked Margarete to speak in private. She said, "Sure." We walked to the small conference room. My legs felt heavy, as it was a long walk to the room. I sensed that she was ready to be informed of bad news. We sat down and she asked, "What do you want to talk to me about?"

I said, "I did not pass the board."

This was probably shocking to her, because of the way I had accomplished so much so far, and it was already proven that I could pass it without any doubt.

She said, "No problem. You just take the next exam. Until then, you work as a physical therapist assistant."

Since Washington state did not have a physical therapist assistant (PTA) licensure, I would automatically qualify to be a PTA. This fact was awfully fortunate for me, because most states require a PTA licensure to legally practice as a PTA under the supervision of a physical therapist. In other words, I could continue working at the Rainier Vista Care Center to provide rehabilitation services.

I now had to let all the staff members know this too, particularly the other three physical therapist assistants, because there were legal issues involved with supervision and in signing off on treatment plans. Although I had had many humiliating moments in my life, this was rough because I had only worked there for four weeks, so I did not know them well.

Contrary to my anxiety, they were considerate, respectful, and kind. First I approached the lead PTA, Donna. She whispered to me, "We still consider you a wonderful physical therapist for us. Don't worry."

That was all I needed to hear. She thoughtfully let all the rest of the therapists know of my new position in the PT Department. As other therapists were informed of my new status, everyone came up to give me encouraging words and respect. I was profoundly moved by their warmth and mature behaviors. This was one of many qualities I liked about living in America—that people had a capacity to accept failures and imperfections, which are major parts of life.

Although I was given eight hours to complete the examination with the magnifying reading monitor in a private room accommodated by the state, I could not pass it for the second time either. Why did I fail it twice? I simply did not have the physical and mental strength to prepare for it and manage the 200 questions while working 40 hours a week.

In the midst of despair, I realized that I was just a few points away from meeting the Washington passing score, and that the score I received actually met most state board standards. So I decided to apply for a Florida physical therapist license. I felt at home there with my many friends and the desirable weather all year, even though it would take me an extra 10 hours to visit my family and friends in Japan. I received my Florida PT license within a month, and I then got busy selecting the best place to work as a physical therapist there.

I explained to Margarete that I would resign after I secured my new employment in Florida. She was very happy for me that I had finally become a physical therapist with a permanent license. I also explained the situation to Claudia. She totally understood how I reached the decision to return to Florida after living in Washington for nearly six months. I felt regretful, though, because she had taken tremendous time and care with me to start my new life in Washington. And, of course, she was the one who gave me the last ride to the airport when I flew back to Florida in April of 1994.

In summary: I chose Washington state to start building my career in a skilled nursing facility. While working there, I failed the state board physical therapist licensure examination twice. However, the score was satisfactory in most other states. As a result, I decided to return to Florida and I was able to start rebuilding my career.

Use Your Applied Faith

Faith is a solid foundation providing you with a place of safety and a source of courage. So having faith allows you to feel free to attempt anything with the expectation of a positive outcome.

Applied faith is positive belief in action. For example, I failed the Washington state PT licensure examination twice. However, I believed that the failure was not an accurate reflection of who I was. After all, I was able to establish a respectable PT career in Florida. Faith helps attract conditions and circumstances you really want. Try to develop faith and self-confidence to believe in yourself.

If people around you have faith in you, they will give you even more power to overcome challenges. Remember professor Karen Fisher and Curl Fernandez, the PT at Jackson Memorial Hospital in Miami, from Chapter 4? They absolutely had faith in me. Can you start cultivating applied faith today? Yes, you can.

Applied faith may be the most difficult concept to understand. But this is the most important element when circumstances become awfully hard. The "Exercises for Your Dream" section will further explain it for you.

Epilogue

In Florida, I worked in the field of geriatric rehabilitation for five years. In 2001, I established
a company that provided continuing education
seminars for physical therapists and physical
therapist assistants. The seminar was titled
"How to Use Acupuncture Points in Physical
Therapy." I traveled through many states to offer
this seminar, which became popular amongst
rehabilitation professionals. I presented this
seminar until 2007.

Since the late 1980s, I had instinctively known
that a serious computer-based world economy
was coming. So I immediately invested time in
formal computer training. Fortunately, Florida
Community College of Jacksonville housed
an institution called Independent Living for the
Visually Impaired (ILVI). The training involved
learning about what a computer was and what
it did. It also included "touch typing" skills. I
struggled with getting used to all the keys on
the keyboard. Improving touch typing was difficult because the program required at least

95 percent accuracy as well as a typing speed of 25 words or more per minute. In addition, I was already 47 years old and definitely showing symptoms of Spinocerebellar Degeneration, which affected my muscles and the strength and coordination of my upper and lower extremities. Around this time, I started to need a cane to walk. I practiced with an old keyboard given to me by the training center, both at home and during my commutes to the ILVI.

It took seven months of going there four days a week in order to pass the entire touch-typing program, starting with typing the "home row position" keys of the left hand. The last phase was to type a 200-word essay with 95 percent or above accuracy while keeping up with the reader's speed on my headset. Regarding accuracy, I had little trouble scoring above 95 percent consistently; however, I had difficulties with increasing my speed. This entire process indeed showed that I placed value in quality, attention to details, and how I achieved a goal.

After completing the computer program, my world expanded. In adulthood, my visual acuity had gone from 20/200 to 20/2000. Through the program, I was given a desktop computer loaded with Microsoft Office and a ZoomText magnification reader program for the visually impaired. As soon as I set it up, it booted up and worked perfectly. I was reaching 50 years of age in couple of years, but inside I was jumping up and down like a child. I was so proud of myself for being able to assemble it. Since I was little, even a simple mechanical procedure, such as driving in a screw, would be done for me because of my visual impairment. This was the typical Japanese sentiment of "I'll just do it for you." Although it appeared to be a kind behavior, it did not help me nurture the self-confidence I greatly needed to figure out how to do things for myself through effort and a little ingenuity in spite of the difficulties in life. I quickly gained confidence in emailing, researching, writing by using Word, and learning various computer functions.

One of the things I really wanted to actualize was to help young Japanese people experience even a small taste of America. I believed that the United States would give them various stimuli and influence their hearts and minds, which would help them navigate their lives from a broader perspective. Therefore, I sought out the help of Dr. Hiroshi Nakamura, a professor at a physical therapy school in Tokyo. We decided to create a program for graduating Japanese physical therapy students to come to Jacksonville, Florida, where I lived. It took about five years to make it a reality.

We wanted it to be a great learning tour; at the same time, it had to be an enjoyable experience for them. So we took the students to one of the largest and most reputable nonprofit health organizations in the southeast region of the United States, Brooks Rehabilitation Hospital. Because we also wanted them to experience a physical therapy school and meet American students, we visited the University of North Florida (UNF) and the University of South Florida (USF). At the end of the learning tour, we always visited the world-renowned Mayo Clinic. After that, it was all fun and leisure. We went to Orlando to experience Universal Studios and Disney World.

We were able to carry out this program four times between 2012 and 2016. I believed that many of the new PT graduates received impactful impressions of American people, hospitalities, cultures, systems, and insights into how they ran businesses, including medical services and higher education. Most of all, the vast lands containing enormous potentials of natural resources and richness impressed them.

We really helped to broaden their horizons. I sincerely hope that we provided them opportunities they would never have had on their own.

In the process of arranging the learning tour during February of 2011, I made an appointment with professor Donnie Welch-Rawls, the director of the UNF PT Clinical Education Program. During the meeting, she mentioned that she was currently going to a doctoral program in physical therapy while working for the university. At that time, physical therapy education was transitioning toward the doctoral program nationwide. She also mentioned that USF would start offering transition into the doctoral program for a period of three years, accepting those candidates who had graduated from a bachelor's or master's program. I felt that would be a great opportunity to upgrade myself for the future.

As soon as I returned home, I called the USF PT school to ask about the transitional doctoral physical therapy (tDPT) program. The secretary explained to me that the application had to be received by the end of August of 2011 for starting on January 2, 2012. She also explained that I needed to submit the official transcripts from all colleges and universities that I attended, the proof of my current Florida physical therapist license, the proof of citizenship or permanent residence of the United States, and two letters of recommendation. I felt that I could satisfy all the requirements. I gave myself a "Go" sign for the doctorate degree in physical therapy.

I immediately began contacting all of my universities for official transcripts and for two people who knew me well enough to write letters of recommendation. Moreover, I wanted to speak with Dr. Williams, the USF doctorate program director, because I would be venturing into an unknown level of education after being away from academic work for almost 20 years. Thus, I needed to explain my visual impairment that required various accommodations to complete the seven semesters of course work.

I left a message with his secretary, and within two hours he called me back. His voice was very clear and strong, as if he was speaking by using all the cells in his body. "I am Dr. Williams. How may I help you?"

I explained my desire to earn a doctorate degree by attending the USF program. At the same time, I explained that I needed accommodations due to my visual impairment. I timidly asked, "Do you think that I could successfully complete the program?"

He replied in an even stronger and more confident voice, "Absolutely, you can. Shiro, I want you to submit your application."

I responded to his encouraging words. "Yes, I will send in my application with all supporting documents." I had no idea how competitive it would be to be accepted into the program. But, once again, I was committed to give it my all and climb another mountain.

Because of my determination and unshakable desire, I received the acceptance letter to the program in early November. By this time in my life, I had learned that I would feel confident achieving my purpose once the opportunity was presented to me. I started the first semester on January 2, 2012, and I completed the program in April of 2014.

By this time I was married and had three children. Here is how I successfully completed the coursework to earn my doctorate degree while raising triplets: First, I contacted the Office of Students with Disabilities about making my textbooks into MP3 audio files so that I could listen to them anywhere without a magnifying reading monitor. I used my time waiting for and riding on community transportation to listen to the textbooks. And I asked one of my friends to download the DVD course lecture into my MP3 player. In other words, my methods of achieving this new level of academic degree were to rely upon audio learning as much as I could. Eventually, I felt that I established a new learning style that was based at least 70 percent on intentional listening.

In the third week of April of 2014, I received probably the last email from Dr. Vorro, who was my doctoral case study advisor teaching anatomy at The Ohio State University. In this program, each student was assigned a professor who was suited for the contents of the student's case study.

If I summarized my life in one word, I would say "proving." Thirty years of my American life was all about proving that I was capable of accomplishing goals that were beyond most people's imagination. So I tried not to reveal to Dr. Vorro that I was visually impaired because I wanted to prove I could jump over this highest and last hurdle by completing my doctoral research paper without special accommodations. Yes, I was risking not receiving the degree that I had worked diligently for over the past six semesters.

I was determined to successfully complete this most challenging final 16 weeks. One of the best strategies was to readily follow Dr. Vorro's advice. For instance, I had to send him each paragraph that I completed. He examined the style and size of the words, and told me how to notate numbers, initials, references, etc. He also specified how to email him and write the cover page. After all that discipline, and no encouraging words, he finally recognized my sincere endeavor and honorable challenge by saying, "Your research was well-written." At the end of his email, he wrote, "Shiro, Congratulations!"

The grade posted was 100 percent. I was overwhelmed with joy and a sense of pride because I had successfully completed my most difficult semester without any special accommodations. In other words, I had gained invaluable confidence that I could compete with others under the same conditions. After the official announcement of completion of the program, I found that our class, which had started with 22 doctoral candidates, had only 14 graduates. By this time, I was using two white support canes to walk.

The next day, I called my 89-year-old mother to inform her that I had earned my doctor of physical therapy and rehabilitation sciences degree. More importantly, I posed the question that I could not ask her for the past 30 years. I built up my courage and asked, "Did you think that I could accomplish what I said I would and come this far?"

She immediately replied, "I absolutely believed you could do it."

As soon as she said it, tears welled up in my eyes. I could no longer speak with her. I just said, "I will call you later." I felt that she knew that I was teared up. I was exhausted and sat down on my desk chair. I thought that my mother was great. She had probably known and believed in everything about me since I was born. *Thank you, mother.* Again, it was another moment that I felt my mother's greatness and love.

My life has been truly unique and beyond my wildest dreams. If I did it again, I would not change much of anything. I have to give myself a "passing" grade for my adventurous and honest life of 30 years in the United States.

Exercises for Your Dream

Chapter 1: Definite Purpose (Life's Work)

One of the most difficult self-assignments is to identify and decide on what worthwhile purpose you want to spend the best period of your life pursuing. For example, my definite major purpose was to become a physical therapist in the United States. I believed this challenging choice would create invaluable worldly experiences and provide me with an enriching, ideal life.

1. Ask yourself this question: *What is the most ideal life for me?*
2. If you agree with your most ideal life in your imagination, go for it. It will be challenging, but so rewarding, joyful, and unforgettable.
3. Once you have identified your ideal life, you can easily determine a second-best and a third-best life, to provide you with flexibility. But do not grab the low-hanging fruit.
4. Make a movie in your mind showing the heroic ending scene of your most ideal life.

5. Once you find it, write it down in words and paste it somewhere you will see it every day. You may draw yourself with a winning smile.

6. Write down all the advantages of having a definite purpose. For example, it develops self-reliance, self-confidence, creative imagination, faith, integrity, and so on.

7. Tell people you can trust about your definite purpose, including how enthusiastic you are. This will give you an extra responsibility or promise that you must do your best to attain your dream.

Chapter 2: Desire

Desire is your driving force to attain your definite purpose. It is the consistent flow of energy that takes root from highly emotionalized thoughts, such as faith, love, sex, traumatic or touching experiences, or a combination of multiple feelings. Desire can be so strong that it fully commits you to moving unerringly toward your dream.

1. You already have something in your past or present experiences, or even your future

concerns, that you feel very strongly about. Find a way to use that source of emotional energy for attaining your dream. There is a good chance that you already have those strong emotions to move yourself toward the definite purpose.

2. Control and contain that highly emotion-alized source of power for positive use instead of igniting a fire that can hurt your-self or others.

3. Once you have tied your definite pur-pose with your burning desire, you have the main qualities for a winning formula.

4. Write down your desire and read it aloud; quietly tell yourself daily that you will possess it, because success is very shy and timid.

5. Desire will bring success unless you recognize failure.

Chapter 3: Organized Planning

An intelligent and deliberate plan is necessary to reach your definite purpose. For instance, I often convince myself that "99 percent of life is preparation." Your success depends on strategizing your actions for attaining your major purpose.

1. Obtain as much detailed information as possible about what you are trying to do.

2. Understand and analyze this information to determine the logical order in which you should take actions.

3. Carry out the actions by "assembling alliances" and "going the extra mile" with a positive attitude and flexibility for unexpected events.

4. Make a schedule sheet for your plans with details of when they are to be finished, with what level of quality, and so on. It is better to be as concrete as possible.

Chapter 4: Persistence

Persistence is the continued endeavor to keep overcoming challenges, even if there are still many in front of you. This process requires enormous physical and mental energy and endurance, which comes from a full commitment to your definite purpose and a burning desire to complete it. You can cut down a giant oak tree by swinging your axe only once a day. Eventually the tree will fall. So don't give up. Keep swinging.

1. Your definite purpose is major and significant enough that your motivation will sustain your efforts to reach your dream.
2. Well-organized planning will help you go through difficulties along the way.
3. No matter what, keep up with that definite action to move forward, even just one millimeter every day.
4. If you persist with your honest efforts and integrity, the world will be compelled to reward you.

Chapter 5: Cooperative Efforts

Cooperative effort means to work with others to achieve your definite purpose. One individual's abilities alone may not succeed. However, two or more people together, in a spirit of harmony, can produce results beyond your wildest imagination. For example, Apple wouldn't be Apple without Steve Wozniak; Microsoft wouldn't have become Microsoft without Paul Allen; Google might not be Google without Sergey Brin. You need someone you can profoundly trust as you begin your journey for your dream.

1. Again, you must have a definite purpose that presents a power that will convince people to become your strong advocate and equal partner behind the stage.

2. If you are serious, you will be taken seriously. If you want to earn trust from someone you want to give your trust to, you must demonstrate your full commitment to your definite purpose, as well as your respect and loyalty to him or her.

3. How can you meet such a dependable partner? Don't worry; if you have an unwavering purpose with a burning desire to achieve it, like-minded people will come to you.

4. Believe in yourself. The universe will be on your side.

Chapter 6: Positive Attitude

A positive attitude is the single most important quality of the science of success. Whatever you choose to pursue in life, you cannot produce the maximum result without it. This is because you need people to help you to reach your dream. If you are negative, people will not be interested in associating with you. Some people naturally have a positive manner and tone of voice, but some do not. Since the benefits are immeasurable, let's polish and develop your positive attitude.

1. "Think big!" Your definite purpose is so major that you understand there is a difficult journey ahead of you.

2. This mindset will allow you to take hardships with optimism, bridging to the next positive step.

3. You will inevitably experience temporary defeats and failures. However, every such experience will bring a seed of benefits that give you a reason to smile and look forward to the next sunrise.

4. A positive attitude will attract the right circumstances and people for your success. It will also nurture sound health, a labor of love, peace of mind, enduring friendship, freedom from self-limitation, and wisdom to empathize with yourself and others.

5. Observe and study someone who exhibits a positive attitude.

6. Pick the one quality that you desperately need to become more positive and practice it every day. For instance, in the morning, I practice smiling after brushing my teeth in front of the mirror. Then I tell myself aloud, "You look great! It's going to be another wonderful day!"

7. Engage in conversations with thoughtfulness and a good sense of humor.

8. Listen more than you speak. If you give 100 percent of your attention for even a few seconds to others during a conversation, you will make a positive impression. Most people are busy thinking of what to say next instead of trying to give you their maximum attention. Remember, one of the deepest human desires is to be understood.

9. You can only gain a positive attitude by trying wherever and whenever you can. So start practicing it for your bright future.

Chapter 7: Applied Faith

Applied faith is an unshakable spiritual thought that has a practical use for your place of safety and source of courage.

Faith helps you overcome adversity, failure, and temporary defeat. To do anything in life, practical application of a belief is absolutely necessary for attaining your dream.

1. You do not have to be a religious person to be faithful. You can decide what to use as an anchoring system for your place of safety and source of courage. For example, you might believe in the words you were given by your parents or teachers; or maybe you were moved by lessons you learned from well-known quotes, proverbs, and tales.

2. Once you have an anchoring system with other principles, you may become so indomitable that success shall willingly come to you.

3. The good news is that your applied faith will help in your pursuit of happiness for all your life.

Applied faith can be a difficult concept to grasp. Here is my last story to see if it will help you understand how faith positively influenced my life, creating an anchoring system as a place of safety and source of courage.

March 1978

Mr. Makoto Sakaguchi

When I was senior in high school, I truly enjoyed a physics class. This was because the teacher, Mr. Sakaguchi, did not teach us the subject so that we would score well on a test or enter one of the best colleges. He wanted us to be moved by learning about the greatness that many physicists, such as Galileo, Newton, and Einstein, exhibited as enormous contributors for mankind. He certainly succeeded in not only getting us at least interested in physics, but also teaching us not to lose sight of the forest for the trees.

Throughout the academic year, the class was held twice a week, and class was two periods combined. So we had plenty of time to speak about subjects other than physics. For instance, we asked him about his struggle during the two years he kept failing his entrance examination into the best industry and technology university in Japan, similar to MIT. One time we asked him how he met and married his wife. He was always willing to share his life experiences and his honest feelings. The best thing about spending those hours with him was hearing his dramatic and fascinating stories. Probably, he figured that those stories were more impactful than remembering "F=ma."

On the last day of class, those two class periods had nothing to do with physics. Mr. Sakaguchi said, "All the sciences, sports, arts, hobbies, schools, and everything else are merely tools for us to become better human beings. Sometimes we are so caught up with who did better than someone else on a test. From today on, I want every one of you to develop a global or cosmic scale of perspective in life."

Finally, Mr. Sakaguchi sent us away with parting words for each person in the class. I was sure that I would be told lots of ways to improve, especially since I was the first student to attempt to enter a college from our high school for the blind. Besides, my grades at the school for the blind were just okay, not outstanding. I was getting nervous waiting for my turn to be given the comments, because four of my physics classmates who were academically far superior to me had received "improvement" comments.

At last, my turn came and I was the last person to receive comments. I literally felt myself shrinking to the floor until I was about two inches tall. I almost covered both ears with my hands as if I wanted to scream, "I don't want to hear them." Mr. Sakaguchi's voice was warm and a little playful. He smiled at me in the same manner he did with everyone else. "Mr. Iwae," he said softly, "you don't have to change anything. Be just the way you are." His affirmative statements lifted me up on a cloud. I sincerely felt that all 18 years of my life had significance. I suddenly arose with confidence and hope for my future—not just the immediate future, but the big future, although I did not yet know when it would happen.

Now, more than four decades later, I am fundamentally the same person I was when Mr. Sakaguchi gave me that warm and honest encouragement. I have believed his magical words and I have succeeded in both academic and professional careers in the United States. I have somehow met people who gave me inspiration, opportunities, and encouragement that propelled me forward because of Mr. Sakaguchi's simple but powerful affirmation of "You don't have to change anything. Be just the way you are."

Only two years later, at the age of 30, he passed away from a subarachnoid hemorrhage. The only regret I have in my life is that I cannot tell him how his words supported and anchored me so firmly that I have come this far, and that they will be the anchoring system for the rest of my life.

"Thank you very much, Mr. Sakaguchi."

You already possess an extraordinary power in your mind. Use it to the highest level for you and others in the world.

Thank you very much for having read this book. I hope that it gave you an enriching experience.

If you have comments, please contact me at:

Shiro Iwae, PT, DPT
Author, Physical Therapist, Education Reform Consultant
Website: https://driwae.com
Email: shiro@driwae.com

Acknowledgments

First, I have to express my appreciation to these two people: the Hall of Fame speaker, Lou Heckler, who introduced me to the business book strategist, Cathy Fyock. She recognized a potential in my story and provided me with proper guidance, including impressive praise as well as encouragement to produce a book. I am also grateful to the Ignite Press team members who assisted me in creating the actual physical and digital products. I thank my triplet children—William, Garrett, and Yvonne—for being so inspirational that I was able to complete the book. I am forever thankful to Howard and Doris Keim in Oklahoma, who gave me the courage, hope, and belief that I could become a physical therapist in the United States. I give heartfelt thanks to all the volunteers and friends who enriched my life. And I appreciate my grandmother, Tsuru Iwae, who always watched out for me, and was my unshakable and immovable Northern Star in the sky. Finally, I must honor my mother, Tomiko Iwae, who truly believed in my abilities and possibilities since I was born and continued to believe in me after I was diagnosed with optic neuropathy, meaning that I would be legally blind for the rest of my life. I must give many thanks to countless other people who helped me along the way. You have made me who I am today. You keep me grounded and you own a piece of my memory.

Review Inquiry

I hope you've enjoyed the book, finding it both useful and fun. I have a favor to ask you.

Would you consider giving it a rating wherever you bought the book? Online book stores are more likely to promote a book when they feel good about its content, and reader reviews are a great barometer for a book's quality.

So please go to the website of wherever you bought the book, search for my name and the book title, and leave a review. If you are able, perhaps consider adding a picture of you holding the book. That increases the likelihood your review will be accepted!

Many thanks in advance,
Shiro Iwae

Would You Like Shiro Iwae to Speak to Your Organization?

Book SHIRO IWAE Now!

Shiro Iwae accepts a limited number of speaking/coaching/training engagements each year. To learn how you can bring his message to your organization, email shiro@driwae.com or visit https://driwae.com.

About the Author

After becoming an acupuncturist with some training in rehabilitation in Japan, Dr. Shiro Iwae worked for a hospital as a physical therapist assistant. There he met a supervising physical therapist who possessed superior professional and people skills. Dr. Iwae was profoundly moved by how he worked harmoniously with patients as well as colleagues. He decided to become a physical therapist who inspired people just as this person did for him.

Although diagnosed as legally blind at the age of four, Dr. Iwae had the mindset of "If I invest my precious youthful time for the future, I will do it in a way that no one else has done it before, and it must be challenging enough to test my highest abilities."

As a result, he became a well-respected physical therapist and earned a doctorate degree in rehabilitation sciences from the College of Medicine at the University of South Florida. Receiving an American education gave him tremendous opportunities and confidence. As he looks back on his life, he truly feels that he lived and fulfilled every minute of it.

Now in the last third of his life, he is actively engaged in speaking opportunities, especially to encourage young Japanese people to have more of an "abundant mentality" and less of a "scarcity" in their thoughts. He also likes to participate in philanthropic work to improve the "gender gap index" in Japan. He hopes to be active for life.

Shiro Iwae can be reached at email: shiro@driwae.com and website: https://driwae.com.